Football Babylon 2

Football
Babylon 2

Russ Williams

First published in Great Britain in 1998 by
Virgin Books
an imprint of Virgin Publishing Ltd
Thames Wharf Studios
Rainville Road
LONDON W6 9HT

A catalogue record for this book is available from the British Library.

ISBN 0 7535 0211 9

Typeset by TW Typesetting, Plymouth, Devon

Printed and bound by
Mackays of Chatham PLC, Lordswood, Chatham, Kent

TO MUM

Thanks for everything and more

Contents

Acknowledgements

Special thanks to Michael and Nigel at MPC, Alex, Jim and Clive at Deadline Features (again!), Ben at Virgin, David Willis in Singapore, Richard and the team at *TF* magazine and Osasu Obayiuwana. Also, thanks to those people who wish to remain anonymous – without you, *Football Babylon 2* would not have been possible. Lastly, grateful thanks to Julia Biddle for making sense of my handwritten copy.

Introduction

Football Babylon was published in the autumn of 1996 and catalogued the history of sleaze and corruption in world football. From the origins of football through to the present day, the book covered over a century of scandal. Prolonged sales turned it into a surprise bestseller, fuelled by the most powerful marketing tool of them all – word of mouth. Fans have both a desire to learn more about the game's seedier side and a right to expect the game to be as clean as possible. From sex scandals to bungs, intimidation to drug abuse, agents' tales to court cases, *Football Babylon* covered the whole range of footballing sins. Of course, names were withheld to protect the guilty (and the lawyers).

Football Babylon 2 picks up where the first book left off, continuing on the central theme but expanding the perimeters. African football is closely examined, largely due to the continent's emergence as a footballing power. However, growing credibility is more down to raw talent than design and organisation. Witch doctors and muti men play a large part in the African game, as does exploitation and the use of political manipulation to affect the outcome of football matches.

The influence of illegal bookmakers controlled by triad

gangs in south-east Asia is cause for concern in European football, particularly in the English game. These well-organised gangs would love to control English football to the degree that they have the Asian game. Some people claim that the syndicates have already achieved their objectives. Just how far have their tentacles of corruption spread? What can we do about it? Can we stop it?

Even more names have been withheld to protect the guilty and you will soon see why. European football comes under the spotlight again, as does the game around the rest of the world, with tales of violence, drug abuse, intimidation, corruption and a whole host of other sins from some unlikely sources. The usual suspects appear as well, especially in the chapter that chronicles footballers' obsessions with gambling. In general, British players gamble much more than any of their European counterparts. Yes, it is part of our British culture, but once hooked, individuals find it very difficult to stop their habit from escalating to alarming levels – and it can lead to suspicion from fans. Reading in the paper that a player has bet on a match in which he is participating does not exactly inspire confidence.

Supporters often complain that they are not appreciated by the clubs they follow. It's all too easy to take their money and pay lip service to their views. Any club chairman that may have underestimated the dedication of a club's fans need look no further for proof of their conviction than Chapter 7 – extraordinary stories of faith, despair, dedication and, to be frank, unhealthy obsessions.

You would be forgiven for thinking that Brazilian football is all about breathtaking skill and winning World Cups. In fact, it is among the most corrupt in South America. The Argentinian League is home to the most violent derby match in the world, and deaths among supporters are a regular occurrence.

Spain's Jesus Gil makes Chelsea's outspoken Ken Bates look like a pussy-cat. He will stop at nothing to achieve his objectives, even if it means breaking the rules. Portuguese football, too, has had its fair share of scandal in the last few years, notably through the bribing of referees.

Exploitation, superstition, abuse, violence and underworld crime all have a part to play in *Football Babylon 2* – an eye-opening account of the maelstrom that is world football. As for *Football Babylon 3*, it's too early to say, but human nature being what it is, I would not rule it out.

1 Europe

SINCE THE PUBLICATION of *Football Babylon*, Europe has continued to excel itself in footballing impropriety. The last 30 months have been littered with bribery, punch-ups, deaths, scandal and deceit. That is not to say that all football is corrupt, but the usual suspects do seem to have the ability to reincarnate themselves and bring some new friends to the party as well.

In direct contrast to the British game, missile throwing is almost a game within a game for some continental supporters. In England, the occasional coin is thrown at a game and hand-held mini lasers, used to impair the vision of players at crucial moments, became worryingly common for a time. Foodstuffs have also made an appearance – notably a shower of hundreds of Mars Bars thrown at Paul Gascoigne upon his return to his former club, Newcastle United, when he was playing for Tottenham in the late 1980s. Much more sinister and not at all funny is the throwing of bananas at black players.

Further afield, the Italians enjoy nothing more than showing their displeasure with players and officials by pelting them with missiles. At a time when football hooliganism appears to be relatively under control in Britain, the Italian police have reported an upsurge in the problem in recent years. Fans attending Serie 'A' matches are now frisked for potential weapons and missiles at the turnstiles, forcing any determined thugs to be a little more resourceful. In February 1997, the Reggiana 'Ultras' (hardcore fans) lost their temper at the home derby against Parma. Frustrated at their team's record of just one home League victory all season, and annoyed as the game was heading towards an uninspiring 0-0 draw, they headed for the Stadio Giglio toilets. Soon after, Parma keeper Luca Bucci's penalty area was covered in plumbing. The local police recovered several kilos of metal pipes and a bathroom tap.

A couple of months later, when Arrigo Sacchi took AC Milan to Naples, an emotional Neopolitan showed his displeasure by hurling an overflowing sack of rubbish towards the former Italian national coach. Sacchi managed to side-step the treat, avoiding the ignominy of trundling into a mound of congealed pasta and half-eaten pizzas. In December 1996, Udinese fans pelted a referee with snowballs when Verona scored a winning goal five minutes into injury time. A linesman in Venice was knocked senseless by an orange at a Serie 'B' game, and Vicenza were fined in 1997 when coins thrown from the home support section injured the referee and both his assistants.

Goalkeepers often walk the missile gangplank, with one of the unluckiest being Otto Konrad, Real Zaragoza's No. 1, who was cracked on the head by a bottle in Milan's San Siro Stadium two years ago while playing for Casino Salzburg. More recently, while playing for Zaragoza, Konrad was hospitalised with first degree burns round his eyes. He had been hit in the face by a firecracker at Bilbao during a Spanish League game.

Cigarette lighters and stadium seat cushions are the preferred missiles of Spanish fans. They are also keen water bottle throwers, as in Italy, where the authorities and the police never seem especially bothered about the dozens of plastic bottles hurled at players when they are taking corners. One Racing Lens fan overstepped the mark in 1997, however, when at a French League match against Paris St Germain, play was suspended because a 1.5 litre bottle of Evian had almost decapitated a linesman.

Inevitably, match officials are common targets for football's lunatics. One Spanish referee was shot in the arm by a pitch-side sniper hiding in a forest. Another nutcase chucked a live snake at a referee during a Bulgarian League match and a furious woman spectator ran on to the pitch and attacked referee Rob Hass in a local match in Vienna. Well, the man in black *had* sent her husband off!

Napoli fans took direct action to new heights in November 1997. Unhappy at their team's performance in Serie 'A' and the prospect of relegation, they simply set fire to the stadium when Napoli lost 4-0 at home to Parma. A mob of fans then tried to reach the home team dressing room to emphasise their unhappiness. Napoli coach, Giovanni Galeone, said, 'I can understand their anger. The fans who care behave like a lover who has been betrayed. When that happens, people insult each other and it can lead to shooting or stabbing.' Oh, that's OK, then.

In 1997, football almost presented the divided island of Cyprus with a breakthrough. Then politics intervened. Three days before the first of two historic football matches that would have ended 42 years of sporting division between the north and south of Cyprus, age-old political squabbling surfaced again. After fourteen months of secret meetings and negotiations, the games were called off, and each side blamed the other for scuppering the FIFA-sponsored initiative.

The official Greek Cypriot Football Association said that they called off the Under-18 games that had been scheduled for 12 and 19 June 1997 because they were unhappy with a letter sent by the north to FIFA. The crux of the problem was that the north called themselves the 'Cyprus Turkish Football Association', which according to Cypriot FA president Marios Lefkaritis meant, 'We should recognise two football associations in Cyprus. We reject this.

'Another important issue was the procedure of how we would go to the occupied areas for the game in the north. We were not willing to accept immigration procedures.'

The first game had been scheduled for the Greek side, with the return match a week later in North Nicosia. The wording of the letter may have been viewed as trivial by some people but as far as the Greek Cypriots were concerned, it was a crucial issue in their struggle not to give credence to the island's partition. The Turks viewed the games as a stepping stone to some form of international recognition.

The Turks were furious that in the letter to FIFA, the Greeks had described a village in the Turkish north as 'occupied Laptibus'. Ilgun Ustan, vice-president of the unofficial Northern FA, said, 'There are no occupied towns in northern Cyprus. We regard such references as provocative and politically motivated. As for the title of our Football Association, if it's good enough for FIFA, why isn't it good enough for the Greeks?'

In the complicated and often petty world of Cypriot politics, football *almost* managed to bring a divided island together. After negotiations were formally abandoned, one

Greek Cypriot official commented, 'We didn't want the Turkish Cypriots to take advantage. We have taken a brave step forward but it seems that things have turned the other way.' FIFA asked both sides to try again.

The chances are that if the game *had* gone ahead, there would have been a politically fuelled pitch battle between the players and the whole thing would have ended in tears. There have been a couple of notable pitch battles between players in English football over the last couple of seasons. On 22 February 1997, Chesterfield met Plymouth at Saltergate. The man in black on duty that day was Richard Poulain, who went into the football history books as the first man in 109 years of League football to send off five players in one game. Undeniably, the 'Battle of Saltergate' was a deplorably violent match. Plymouth's Ronnie Mauge was given his marching orders after 36 minutes and with ten minutes to go, the score 2-1 to the visitors, the referee's afternoon looked as if it would end quietly. In fact, it had hardly begun. At a corner kick, Chesterfield's Darren Carr slid into Plymouth keeper Bruce Grobbelaar, leaving him concussed and his team-mates incensed. All hell let loose as a series of punches were thrown. Chesterfield's Kevin Davies came to blows with Richard Logan on the six-yard line while Carr ran into Plymouth defender Tony James in the goal mouth. Fourteen other players pushed, shoved and punched each other around the penalty spot, while supporters, stewards and the Plymouth bench spilled on to the pitch. When it evetually died down, two players from each side were shown red cards – Chesterfield's Carr and Davies and Plymouth's Logan and James. After the game, Mr Poulain said, 'I've never seen anything like that. It was totally unexpected. I just flew back from a holiday last night – now

I'll need another one to get over that. It was frightening, really.'

Plymouth's caretaker manager, Mick Jones, commented: 'I'm not complaining about the ref . . . It's possible I might have pumped up my players a little too much.'

The third round of the FA Cup was shamed on 3 January 1998 at Barnsley's ground, Oakwell. The home side were playing Bolton Wanderers in what is often referred to as the best knock-out competition in the world, although knock-out was interpreted slightly differently on this occasion. It was a fiercely competitive game and in the dying seconds, Bolton's Neil Cox chased a ball that had gone out of play. The Barnsley bench were slow to return the ball and Cox was less than impressed. He pushed the nearest person to him, provoking Barnsley's Eric Winstanley to shove Cox in the back. Within seconds, every player on the field was reacting to an opponent, right in front of the dug outs. The substitutes and management of both teams waded in, as did stewards and police. Scott Sellars, Georgi Hristov, Andy Todd, Ashley Ward and Jamie Pollock were all seen scrapping. Pollock was allegedly on the receiving end of a vicious right hander from one of the stewards, who was arrested but later released.

The incident was, however, short lived, and referee David Elleray said, 'I saw very little of what was happening and I didn't see anything I should report.' (Perhaps that explains some of his decisions on the pitch . . .!) He added that, 'Nothing untoward had happened. It was a typical English Cup tie. I enjoyed it.'

One of Spanish football's most colourful characters is Atletico Madrid's controversial president, Jesus Gil. On 25 April 1996, Gil was suspended for ten months by the Spanish

Football Federation as punishment for striking the general manager of Compostela. The incident happened when Gil bumped into the Compostela officials outside the Spanish Football League's headquarters. Compostela chairman, Jose Maria Caneda, was accompanied by the club's general manager, Jose Gonzalez Fidalgo, and Jesus Gil saw red when he spotted the pair. The reason for Gil's anger was simple – Caneda had suggested on television that the residents of Marbella, where Gil was mayor, must be mentally unsound to vote for him. The following is an accurate translation of the confrontation. On spotting Caneda, Gil shouted, 'Look, there's the big pork sausage thief who insulted the residents of Marbella and my club. You rob Compostela, and I'll direct my club!'

'Son of a whore,' responded Fidalgo.

'No, you're the son of a whore!' replied Gil.

'The only son of a whore is you, you clown,' argued Fidalgo.

More insults flew, together with some pushing and shoving, and Caneda was heard to shout, 'Don't touch my balls, you tit sucker!'

Gil served his ban but it wasn't long before he was in trouble again, facing charges of racism. In 1997, Atletico Madrid were drawn in the same Champions' League group as Ajax of Amsterdam, and Jesus Gil caused outrage with comments about the number of black players in the Ajax squad. Gil gibbered, 'Those from the Congo and the Antilles – you see them warming up, five blacks there, four there, three more on the field. It looks like the Congo Tome . . . with all respect.'

Gil refused to apologise after the outburst, despite widespread public criticism. He stormed, 'I've never been racist, whatever they say. The colour of the skin is not a sign of racism for me.' He went on, 'Ajax seem marvellous to me. Do I know the players? No, not all of them. There are so many blacks there that I don't know them.'

One player who made his name at Ajax is Patrick Kluivert, who in April 1996 was anxiously awaiting a May Day court appearance in connection with a charge relating to a fatal traffic accident, in which Holland's most famous theatre director was killed. The prosecutor at the trial requested a nine-month jail sentence and the judge initially agreed but later reduced it to a fine and community service. Amazingly, on the day of the victim's funeral, Kluivert committed another traffic offence when he drove through a red light. He was let off with a period of community service and a two-year driving ban.

The following year, Kluivert was back in court after a twenty-year-old woman he had met in an Amsterdam disco accused him of rape. The woman told the court how she had left the disco with Kluivert and three of his friends and was then forced to have sex with them. Kluivert and company pleaded their innocence, arguing that the girl gave her full consent. In court, it was claimed that Kluivert had offered the girl money in return for her silence but she had gone to the police instead. The situation was compounded by the fact that Kluivert's girlfriend was in hospital awaiting the birth of their first child while the Ajax star was appearing in court. Further newspaper allegations surfaced, claiming that Kluivert had used his position as a high-profile sportsman to get charges dropped against one of his friends who had been involved in a violent fight. The rape charge was eventually dropped after the court ruled that there was lack of evidence, with Kluivert and the Dutch FA breathing a collective sigh of relief over the embarrassing allegation.

Portuguese football was embroiled in a massive bribery scandal in 1996 when Fernando Barata, the former chairman of Farense and a millionaire hotelier, accused Porto of paying for a £3,000 holiday for a referee and his family. Porto chairman, Jorge Pinto Da Costa, claimed the allegations were 'ridiculous and absurd' and that the paid holiday was simply 'an accounting error'. It was not the first time that Da Costa had been accused of trying to influence referees. In 1984, Fernando Barata claimed that he had been approached to be the go-between for the Porto chairman and Romanian referee Ion Igna. Barata said that Igna was offered £30,000 to fix a Cup Winners' Cup match between Porto and Aberdeen, a game which Porto won 1-0. 'Pinto Da Costa knew that I had very good contacts with Romania through business and that's why he asked me to fix the Porto–Aberdeen game,' said Barata. Both Porto and the referee escaped an official police inquiry into the charges as the Portuguese law against corruption in sport only came into force in 1991 and could not be used retrospectively.

Da Costa has been regularly accused of bribing referees in his quest to see Porto in an equal position with the two giant Lisbon clubs, Benfica and Sporting. There has never been any concrete proof of wrongdoing as far as Porto are concerned, but there has been much rumour and counter rumour. It has to be said, however, that the standard of refereeing in Portugal over recent years has been variable at best. Jorge Pinto Da Costa offers his own views. 'People talk about us influencing and bribing referees. Before they talked like that, they spent a long time suggesting that our players were doped.' A lot of people take what Da Costa has to say with a pinch of salt. Known as 'the Godfather' in Portugal, outside Oporto he is a universally hated figure. Since he took control of Porto in 1982 they have won eight Championships, four Portuguese Cups, one European Cup and one World Club Championship. Perhaps success breeds jealousy, but in this particular case, many people would beg to differ.

The first allegations against him were made by SIC, Portugal's leading independent TV channel. In November 1996, SIC revealed that FC Porto picked up the £3,000 tab for a luxury Brazilian holiday taken by Portugal's top referee, Carlos Calheiros and his family. Hot on the heels of that allegation came the publication of an off-the-record interview with former Porto – and national – coach Antonio Oliviera, in which he admitted his involvement in 'one of the biggest scandals in the history of Portuguese football' – the use of forged papers to sign Zairean player, N'Dinga. Corruption is a big problem in Portuguese football and the nation's three daily sports papers are characteristically vigilant in their pursuit of the truth. On 20 November 1996, a court in Oporto sentenced former referee Jose Guimaro to fifteen months in prison for accepting a bribe of £2,000 from one of the city's clubs, LECA FC. The club president, Manuek Lopes Rodrigues, was also jailed for a year for his part in the scandal. Police investigations into wrongdoing in Portuguese football are frequent and in-depth. With a number of corruption charges pending, time will only tell if the investigations are successful.

But Portugal is by no means alone. Bribery and match fixing appears to be common throughout the football world, leaving very few countries untouched. Eyebrows were raised in December 1996 when Cyprus lost 3-1 at home to Bulgaria in a World Cup qualifier. In January 1997, accusations that the match had been rigged were made. The Cypriot FA called for an investigation into bookmakers' records to discover how much money had been bet on the home side to lose. The local media claimed that players in the Cypriot team bet heavily on their side to lose, resulting in Bulgaria winning so easily. One British bookmaker on the island, Victor Chandler, scoffed at the reports. He had noticed no unusual betting patterns among players or punters, he said. Cyprus FA chairman, Marios Lefkaritis, had other ideas. 'What concerns us is that the integrity of football is at stake. We are trying to collect as much information as possible from betting shops to see what kind of amounts were at stake.'

The Cypriot authorities believe that up to £40,000 in bets were staked on an away win – roughly five times what was normally gambled. In previous matches, Cyprus had beaten Israel 2-0 and Israel had beaten Bulgaria 2-1, so it was by no means a dead cert that the Bulgarians would win. Nothing was proved beyond reasonable doubt although heavy suspicion remained, with Cypriot FA vice-chairman Costas Koutsokoumnis virtually saying as much. 'I can only say the performance of some players was not as it normally is in other games.'

The Albanian government banned all football matches on 29 January 1997 in the wake of the unrest over the collapse of the pyramid selling schemes. Caught up in the ensuing chaos was Mario Kempes, 1978 Argentinian World Cup winner, who became coach of Albanian club Lushnja, based 30 miles south of the capital Tirana, in December 1996. The father of the president of Lushnja ran one of Albania's biggest pyramid selling schemes, which meant the club was able to pay Kempes around £10,000 a month – a fortune in poverty-stricken Albania. Following Kempes' arrival, Lushnja were struggling in tenth place in the Albanian league but the club president, Pellumb Xhaferri, confidently predicted, 'In five years' time Lushnja will be one of the top eight clubs in Europe.'

Only two weeks after that bold statement, the immensely popular pyramid schemes which promised vast profits collapsed, bringing financial and social chaos to Albania. Pellumb Xhaferri's father's system ran into difficulties and £90 million worth of its assets were frozen by the finance ministry, leading to violent protests inside the Lushnja Stadium, with the angry mob beating up the country's foreign minister and the riot police. Mario Kempes only decided to leave Albania when the government banned all sporting events during the crisis. 'There's nothing I can do about all this,' he sighed.

It was decided that they would have to improvise on the 1996/97 Championship and a play-off was organised between SK Tirana and Flamurtari. The game was abandoned after it degenerated into violent chaos, and the match was later awarded to SK Tirana by default.

The start of the 1997/98 Albanian season started one day late as a mark of respect to Mother Theresa, who was of Albanian extraction and died in September 1997. From then on, the season progressed normally with no reports of the events of September 1997, until Teuta midfielder Artan Koka, 25, was shot dead as he left the local stadium after training. The motive for the killing was never clear and never discovered.

Former Manchester United player Eric Cantona was very critical of international referee Kurt Roethlisberger after his performance while refereeing Manchester United's Champions' League tie against Galatasaray in Istanbul. Cantona had no qualms about accusing Roethlisberger of having been bribed to make unjust calls in favour of the Turks. 'I am certain that referees have been bought in the European Cup. I ask myself whether Mr Roethlisberger has not also been bought,' said Cantona in an interview with French sports paper, *L'Equipe*. Many saw the Frenchman's comments as sour grapes but his opinion certainly gained some credibility following FIFA's decision to impose a life ban on Roethlisberger for 'attempting to influence' the result of the 1996 Champions' League match between Grasshoppers and French champions Auxerre. UEFA said that twelve days before the match, scheduled for 30 October 1996, Roethlisberger visited Grasshoppers general manager, Erich Vogel, at the club offices.

'Mr Roethlisberger asked whether Grasshoppers would be interested in the referee of the Grasshoppers–Auxerre match on 30 October 1996 not giving decisions against Grass-hoppers,' claimed UEFA. The favour clearly involved money and the sum of 100,000 Swiss francs (about £50,000) was mentioned. Mr Vogel reported the conversation to UEFA, fearful that he was being set up in an elaborate 'sting' operation. According to him, Roethlisberger claimed he was on very friendly terms with the match referee and that it would be easy to arrange the matter. UEFA launched a five-month investigation into the affair, which resulted in a life ban for Roethlisberger and suspension of the match referee, Vadim Zhuk, from international matches. A UEFA spokesman said, 'Through his action Kurt Roethlisberger has violated principles which are indispensable for sport – namely those of loyalty, integrity and sportsmanlike conduct. It is an extremely reprehensible and regrettable case of the entire footballing movement.' Swiss teacher Roethlis-berger vowed to fight the ban through the legal system, saying that his reputation had been damaged by spurious claims from Grasshoppers. He admitted to Vogel's claims but argued that he was only testing how Grasshoppers would react to such an offer. 'I won't allow my name to be dragged through the mud in this way. Everybody who knows me would laugh at this. It's a shocking thing to say. Throughout my life, I have stood for fair play and the standards of a gentleman. Nobody would dream of trying to buy me. They know what my answer would be.'

Yet everybody who knows him would also know that controversy has followed Roethlisberger throughout his career. At the 1994 World Cup finals in the USA, he was pilloried for denying the Belgian team a clear penalty in their second-round clash against Germany, which they lost 3-2. Admitting that he 'made a mistake' in that encounter, he was subsequently barred from officiating in any further USA 94 matches. In 1995 he was said to have abused his position as a Class One FIFA referee while he was campaigning for a seat in the Swiss parliament, a misdemeaour that cost him a three-month ban.

In the early 1990s, Roethlisberger was referee at the 1993 European Cup Final between Marseille and AC Milan at the Olympic Stadium in Munich. The game was swathed in controversy following allegations in 1995 by Jean Pierre Papin, the former Marseille captain who was then playing for Milan, who suggested that three of his Milan team-mates had been bribed. UEFA demanded Papin either provide proof or retract under pain of a long suspension for bringing the game into disrepute. Papin fully retracted what he had said, claiming his comments were taken out of context and were said as a joke.

In 1995, Kurt Roethlisberger was involved in yet more controversy over Switzerland's 2-1 European Championship qualifier victory over Turkey. Roethlisberger claimed that he was asked by reporters from *Blick* newspaper to arrange with the Romanian match referee a positive result for Switzerland. He also said that the journalists were acting with the full support of Rainer Huber, the promotions director of the bank Credit Suisse, the Swiss national team's main sponsor.

The activities of Kurt Roethlisberger forced UEFA president Lennart Johansson to publicly state: 'This could be just the tip of the iceberg.'

In the 1980s, Italian football was rocked by a match-fixing scandal that included some of the country's top stars and history was repeated to a certain degree in 1998. Livorno, leaders of their regional group in Serie 'C1', were threatened with relegation after referee Duccio Baglioni alerted the football authorities to a colleague's attempts at bribery. Many in the Italian game feared that the bad old days were back, with Italian Football Federation president Luciano Nizzola announcing: 'That this has happened in one of the lower divisions is no reason for us to feel complacent about the state of the game at the highest level. Corruption is like cancer. It can spread everywhere.'

The scandal centred around a phone call received by Duccio Baglioni from fellow referee, Divino Ferrarini, who offered him £10,000 to fix a match between Montevarchi and Livorno. Baglioni said that he would think over the offer and asked Ferrarini to call him back. Baglioni alerted the authorities, who made arrangements to record the follow-up call.

When Ferrarini rang back, Baglioni pretended to go along with the deal and quick-thinking League officials appointed a third referee, Feice Strocchia, to travel to the match in secrecy. Officials of the two teams and the referee's assistants were all very surprised when Mr Strocchia turned up instead of Baglioni, who they were told had been injured in training. Montevarchi won 1-0, with Livorno missing a penalty. The day after the match, corruption investigator Biagio Martino arrived on Ferrarini's doorstep to confront him over the situation. Ferrarini was forced to admit his involvement in the scam after hearing a recording of the incriminating phone calls. However, it was not clear who Ferrarini was acting for, although he claimed that he was approached by a mystery man called 'Franco' who was representing a third party. Franco was never traced.

As it is often the case where football corruption is concerned, it is almost impossible to get to the root of the problem. Corrupt parties are experts at covering their tracks although one of the personalities involved did have a track record of corruption. Livorno president Claudio Achilli denied any knowledge of the attempted match fixing, telling journalists: 'It's nonsense. I learned my lesson a long time ago.' He was referring to his three-year ban from football in 1989 for bribing two opposition players when he was president of Pavia. His club were relegated to Serie 'C2' as a punishment when he was found guilty by the Italian FA.

There has been a longheld view in certain footballing circles, particularly at Nottingham Forest, that the 1984 UEFA Cup semi-final between Anderlecht and Forest was fixed. Thirteen years after the event, on 19 February 1997, Anderlecht announced that they had been blackmailed for years over the match and admitted that they had paid 'silence' money to two men – one of them a players' agent, Jean Elst, who claimed to have tapes incriminating Anderlecht. Over £750,000 was paid by the club over a period of four years from 1986. Anderlecht's general manager, Michel Verscheren, attempted to stop the blackmailers in 1988 but failed. In 1991, Roger Vanden Stock, an Anderlecht director, found out what had been happening and stopped the payments. He then reported the details to the Belgian Football Federation, who in turn informed UEFA, European football's governing body. Initial inquiries hit the proverbial brick wall and nothing leaked out on the football grapevine. Then in 1995, Elst tried to reactivate the blackmailing by contacting Roger Vanden Stock, who chose to inform the police.

Vanden Stock suddenly found himself in a moral dilemma as his father, Constant Vanden Stock, was president of Anderlecht at the time of the disputed game in 1984.

'Lodging a formal complaint meant exposing a serious misjudgement by my own father,' he said. 'It took him a long time to come to terms with what that meant. But I felt that it was necessary to protect the club, and to see that justice was done for all our sakes – better late than never.'

Anderlecht were vulnerable to potential blackmail because of the events of 1984, when something quite clearly had gone on. Jeant Elst was the first protagonist to go public and attempt to sell his side of the story to the press. Belgian papers were reluctant to print it but he did have some success. He went public with his accusations about Anderlecht on a radio show, claiming he had paid the 1984 referee, Emilio Guruceta, £750 on Anderlecht's behalf to fix the match. The revelation caused quite a stir on both sides of the North Sea, and Elst revelled in the publicity, further claiming he and his partner, Rene Van Aecken, received nearly £300,000 from Anderlecht for their blackmailing.

What happened was as follows. In 1984, Nottingham Forest led 2-0 from the first leg at the City Ground and seemed likely to progress to the final, where they would have met Spurs in an all English final. In the return leg in Belgium, Anderlecht scored from a penalty which was awarded in highly dubious circumstances and Forest scored what looked to be a perfectly good goal only for it to be disallowed by the Spanish referee Mr Guruceta. Anderlecht won the game 3-0 to go into the UEFA Cup Final. The Forest players were convinced that the goal they had scored had been a perfectly good one and that the Anderlecht penalty should never have been given.

On 20 February 1997 Jean Elst and Rene Van Aecken were released on bail following their arrest on blackmail charges in connection with the match-fixing allegations. Jean Elst admitted that apart from the Anderlecht–Forest UEFA Cup tie, he had also been asked to try and fix one other match in the UEFA Cup that same season between Banik Ostrava and Anderlecht. Both fixes were attempted on the specific instructions of Anderlecht.

For once, the evidence was overwhelming and UEFA banned Anderlecht from European competition for a year, starting from the next time they qualified to play in Europe. Club chairman Roger Vanden Stock insisted in mid 1997 that the payment to the Spanish referee in 1984, made by his father Constant, was a loan and not a gift. Before UEFA handed out the European ban, UEFA president, Lennart Johansson, implied that Anderlecht could not in fact be punished because the ten-year Statute of Limitations had expired – or so he thought because the relevant papers from the Belgian FA 'had gone missing'.

In September 1997, former Forest players claimed that they were considering suing Anderlecht for £1.5 million over the fixed semi-final. Forest estimated that the defeat cost them £400,000 (the equivalent of £1.4 million today) and club chairman Phil Soar was forthright in his views: 'We feel it is more an ethical and a moral matter than a purely financial one. You can't have hundreds of teams, thousands of players and millions of supporters around Europe watching football matches and wondering if referees can be bribed. But we reserve the right to pursue our own case for compensation. I have spoken to the Forest players involved and they are furious about what happened and feel quite cheated.'

Anderlecht's main sponsors, the Generale Bank, expressed concern over the incident and insisted that they had the right to cancel their contract with the club whenever they wished. As the repercussions surfaced, Nottingham Forest indicated in late 1997 that they may press for a European place at the expense of Anderlecht if the Belgian club should qualify at the end of the season.

The full picture was never seen by the interested parties as an essential part of the jigsaw was missing – Emilio Guruceta, the Spanish referee, who was killed some years earlier in a car crash. However, the memories of the Nottingham Forest players have not been clouded with the passing of time. Former Forest defender Viv Anderson remembers the match well. 'I remember on the night we had a penalty appeal that was very harshly turned down. And then Paul Hart scored in injury time. It was a goal that would have taken us through (on the away goals rule) but it was disallowed. We still don't have a clue why. We tried to get hold of a tape after the game, but we couldn't do that either. Some of the lads remember that there was a lot of activity going on around the referee's room after the game but they thought nothing of it. On the night we felt hard done by. I was surprised by the news, because I just thought the referee had had a bad night. I feel most sorry for players like Paul Hart. I'd won medals in Europe before, but for some of our players this was their last and only chance.'

In the end, justice was done. Anderlecht were found to be match fixers but sadly for Forest there was no second European chance. It is just a pity that it took nearly fourteen years to bring the fixers to justice.

More referee trouble was unearthed in the spring of 1998, a week before the European Cup Winners' Cup quarter-final first leg between Real Betis and Chelsea. The official was supposed to be the Swedish referee Leif Sundell but he was replaced by UEFA because he and his two assistants were seen in the directors' box at the Real Betis–Espanyol match a few days before the European tie. UEFA decreed that their presence was 'ill timed' although they were convinced that Mr Sundell had not acted in an 'appropriate manner'. In an embarrassing statement, UEFA explained that Sundell and his two colleagues had been in southern Spain to officiate at a tournament involving Scandinavian teams and had decided on their own initiative to travel to Seville to see the game. UEFA emphasised that they were not invited by Betis to attend the game. In the past, UEFA had got their fingers burnt over bent referees and decided to act quickly in the case of Mr Sundell and his assistants in order to head off any potential trouble at the pass. Chelsea said they were pleased with UEFA's actions and welcomed the appointment of Atanas Ouzounov, a Bulgarian official, for the game which they went on to win comfortably.

Aside from domestic leagues, the big money spinner for Europe's top clubs is the Champions' League, a competition formed solely to satisfy the craving of European TV companies. Seen by many as a forerunner to a European Super League, stakes are high in the Champions' League and the temptation to profit from it is great.

In 1996, Dynamo Kiev were kicked out of the Champions' League for trying to bribe Spanish referee Antonio Lopez Nieto before a tie with Greek club Panathinaikos. Lopez was offered a pair of his and her's £15,000 fur coats for a favourable dispensation towards the Russians. UEFA also suspended Dynamo Kiev from the Champions' League for a further three seasons, a decision that was later rescinded. Russian football has a tremendous pedigree but in recent years had adopted some of its Western counterparts' bad habits.

Lokomotiv Moscow defender, Igor Tchugainov, tested positive for an illegal drug after the Russian League Cup Final in June 1997. Tchugainov, a Russian international, was chosen for a random drug test after Lokomotiv's win over Dynamo Moscow. Drug testing is not common in Russian football and tests are carried out on an ad-hoc basis. On the occasion in question, the Russian Football Federation asked for a random sample because of the significance of the game. Tchugainov's blood contained Bromanthane but the findings were deliberately withheld from the Russian Football League, the clubs and the public. Realising the implications of a positive test for Tchugainov, a second test was ordered and not surprisingly showed no sign of the drug. This analysis was performed by a group including the Lokomotiv and national team doctors and one laboratory worker. The 'negative' result was authorised and signed by all three testers but some time later the lab worker wrote a note saying that the sample was not from the player at all. The note only surfaced when a Moscow newspaper published rumours of the test rigging and began to investigate the story. The problem was that the lab worker may have been telling the truth but the other test doctors could easily point to the general agreement on the second test results by showing the signed papers which included the certification of the result by everyone present. So Tchugainov did not suffer as a result of the allegations and was picked by Russian manager Boris Ignatiev to play in the first leg of Russia's World Cup in the 1998 play-off match against the Italians. Ignatiev stood resolutely behind the player. 'I have absolutely no doubt that Igor is clean,' he said. The lab worker had plenty.

The Russians were forced into the play-off with Italy after they lost 1-0 to Bulgaria in Sofia in 1997. At a critical moment in the Russian football calendar, a newspaper leak alleged that Russian team officials still owed about £190,000 in bonuses from the 1994 World Cup qualification round and the USA finals. One paper said in its editorial: 'Russian football union officials rake in money even when the team loses everything in sight. We didn't really want to throw this dirt, but the latest defeat by the Bulgarians has exhausted our patience.' Russia's unpredictable president, Boris Yeltsin, stepped into the row and granted an amnesty from the tax crackdown.

Eastern European football has always operated under its own set of rules. The former states of the Soviet Union seem to follow a different agenda to other countries and often clubs and officials take the law into their own hands. A good example is the story of Yuri Pohrebnyak, who in 1997, while head coach of Ukranian strugglers, Metalurg Mariupol, was banned for life for attacking the referee after his side lost 2-1 to Vorskla Poltabva. In a premeditated attack. Pohrebnyak led an angry mob into Vadym Shevchenko's hotel room in the early hours of the morning. The referee suffered rib injuries and a broken nose for his trouble.

Some of the justice dished out to Eastern European sinners is laughable. In 1996, Romanian Division Three winners FC Vega encountered their FA's unique system of punishment after being found guilty of bribing opponents. Initially, they were docked 25 points, ensuring they would not gain promotion, but on appeal the points deduction was reduced to twelve. A third Romanian FA committee overruled both decisions and bizarrely arranged a play-off match between FC Vega and second-placed club, Draobeta. Vega won the game and gained promotion to Division Two, proving you can cheat *and* prosper in Romanian football.

In many respects, the Eastern bloc is football's Wild West – geographically a contradiction in terms, maybe, but a fair representation none the less. The more established European football nations may look on with disdain but in truth they are far from whiter than white themselves. In the last couple of years, both France and Spain have had their fair share of problems. On 1 February 1997, the former joint president of Lille FC, Jaques Aymot, was sentenced to an eighteen-month suspended jail sentence for having paid out cash from an illegal fund. Former coach, Georges Heylans, was given a ten-month suspended prison sentence and a £3,000 fine for accepting the payments. Three days later, Bernard Tapie lost his appeal against an eight-month jail sentence for fixing a Marseille match against Valenciennes in 1993 (see *Football Babylon*). In Spain, Deportivo La Coruna president, Augusto Cesar Lendoiro, was banned by FIFA from all football activities as punishment for taking the Spanish FA to court. The ban was lifted at the beginning of 1998 but Lendoiro was still threatening to sue FIFA in the European Court of Human Rights.

Drugs have never been a major problem in Spanish football, with regular dope testing ensuring that the Spanish game is as 'clean' as it can be. However, the sophistication of the tests and the detailed analysis can lead to problems for players. There are a number of substances that are banned under FIFA rules other than narcotics and performance enhancers. Certain cold and flu remedies contain illegal ingredients, so players have to be extremely vigilant. Oviedo defender, Borja Aguirretxu, failed an after-match dope test in 1997 only to find out that it was the ingredients of his hair restorer tablets that had made him test positive!

Far more serious was the case of Paris St Germain goalkeeper, Bernard Lama, who tested positive for cannabis. He asked for a second urine sample, which also proved positive and led to a ban from playing and his exclusion from the French national team. In May 1997, French striker Stephane Paille had his contract terminated by Scottish Premier League side Hearts after becoming the first player ever to test positive for drugs in Scottish football. Over the border, Barnsley's Dean Jones became the first Premiership player to fail a drugs test in October 1997. The English Football Association handed a three-month ban to Jones, who tested positive for amphetamines at Barnsley's training ground in October. Jones pleaded guilty to the charges at an hour-long hearing at Lancaster Gate. He took the drug in a nightclub on 26 October 1997 and claimed he did it merely to keep himself awake, not to enhance his performance on the field. The FA took a dim view of his actions with FA spokesman, Steve Double, saying, 'The FA take a very serious view of this sort of thing and Jones has been suspended from any sort of football for three months.'

The ban from 17 November 1997 to February 1998, and Jones was full of remorse for his 'very foolish' actions. Barnsley's secretary, Michael Spink, said, 'The player is full of remorse and until now has been a model professional.' Jones was told to make himself available for random drug testing at any time in the future, and should he test positive again, he will be banned for life.

Former England Under-21 international Jamie Stuart tested positive for cocaine and marijuana when the FA's doping control unit visited Charlton's training ground on 17 November 1997. The FA charged Stuart with misconduct and Charlton Athletic suspended him and eventually released him after he became the fourth Charlton player to fail a drugs test in three years. The player claimed that the cocaine had been in a cigarette, and he had smoked it on a Thursday night four days before the random drugs test, without being aware of its contents. The FA engaged the services of Professor David Cowan, director of the Drug Control Centre at King's College, Chelsea, who said the test results indicated that it was highly unlikely that the drug had been taken as Stuart had claimed or within the time frame he had specified.

FA spokesman Steve Double said, 'Stuart believes the cigarettes must have been laced with cocaine without his knowledge. But if it had been taken on the Thursday night, the cocaine dose consistent with Professor Cowan's findings could have been fatal.'

Professor Cowan said that in his view, Stuart took a 'normal' dose of cocaine one or possibly two days before the visit of the FA Doping Control Unit. Steve Double's closing statement at the press conference was as follows: 'Jamie Stuart said he had never knowingly taken cocaine and would not take drugs to enhance his performance. The Commission heard Stuart had been involved in a traumatic family crisis at the time of the incident and decided he should be subject to three months' counselling and rehabilitation during which time his suspension from football will continue. He will appear before the Commission again in three months time for the reports to be assessed. Sentencing will be deferred until that date. In the light of the positive drugs tests at Charlton in recent times and at Charlton's invitation, a delegation from the FA will visit the club in the near future to review its drug education procedures.'

On 21 January 1998, Jamie Stuart had his suspension from football extended for a further three months to undergo more counselling and rehabilitation. He has paid a high price for his indiscretion.

West Bromwich Albion defender, Shane Nicholson, also failed a drug test at his club's training ground in October 1997. His sample revealed traces of amphetamine and he was charged by the FA with misconduct and appeared before a disciplinary committee on 21 November. Nicholson claimed that his drink was spiked while on a night out. Generously, his evidence was accepted and he was let off with a warning.

In February 1998, Nicholson was asked to provide another sample for random testing. He refused, despite having made an undertaking to co-operate with the 'drug busters' at his disciplinary hearing. West Brom immediately suspended him, fined him two weeks' wages and left him out of the team for the home game against Portsmouth the following day. Once again, Steve Double spoke for the Football Association: 'Clearly this is a very serious matter. If a player fails to submit to a test it is a disciplinary measure, although this has never happened before. Back in November

Nicholson agreed to submit to target testing and did provide a sample the first time. We are now awaiting reports from the Sports Council as to exactly what took place.'

For a considerable period of time, English football was plagued with stories of cash bungs between players, clubs, agents and managers. Rumours had been rife for a long time that English football had a serious corruption problem and the FA were forced to set up a bungs inquiry that became protracted and exhaustive in its search for the truth. In January 1998 its findings were published, making charges against the former Nottingham Forest manager, Brian Clough, his assistant, Ronnie Fenton, and former Arsenal scout, Steve Burtenshaw. All three were accused of personally benefiting from the transfer of players. FA spokesman, David Davies, steadfastly announced, 'For too long the image of the national sport has been tarnished by serious allegations. Now charges must be answered. The time has come to bring these matters to a conclusion.'

Brian Clough was charged after investigations into the signing of two non-League players from Leicester United to Nottingham Forest. Neil Lyne and Tony Loughran were transferred in 1989 with a fee of £15,000 for the pair agreed, which was the amount banked by the non-League club. The investigation discovered that Forest actually paid £61,000 and the bung report stated that there was 'direct evidence of a fraudulent arrangement by which Clough and/or Fenton acquired a substantial sum'.

Ronnie Fenton was also charged over the £350,000 transfer fee of Alfie Haaland from Norwegian side Byrne to Forest in 1992. The report said that Fenton received a £45,000 backhander from Rune Hauge, the Norwegian agent who was at the centre of the George Graham case. The bung inquiry followed on from the Terry Venables–Alan Sugar high court case in 1993. Clough's name cropped up during the course of the trial when Spurs chairman Sugar said that Clough 'liked a bung' and received £50,000 as part of the deal that took Teddy Sheringham from Forest to Spurs in 1992. At the time, Clough vigorously denied the allegation and challenged Alan Sugar to repeat it outside of the courtroom. Sugar declined to take up his offer but admitted that he found rumours of bungs very disturbing.

The bungs inquiry lasted three and a half years and was presided over by a three-man team: Robert Reid QC, former Premier League chief executive Rick Parry and football manager Steve Coppell. It was these men who uncovered a 'cult of dishonesty' in football.

The Teddy Sheringham transfer investigation revealed that Ronnie Fenton was found to have received a £50,000 payment at a secret meeting at a Luton hotel in 1992. The inquiry decided not to press charges on the issue, even though it found that some of the money had been used by Fenton to pay for his daughter's wedding.

Steve Burtenshaw was chief scout at Arsenal when George Graham was manager. He was accused of receiving a £35,000 payment two months after John Jensen signed for the Gunners from Danish club Brondby in September 1992. The report concluded: 'We are satisfied the payment derived directly from the transfer fees paid by Arsenal to Brondby in connection with the transfer of Jensen.'

Nottingham Forest were accused of making illegal payments and of failing to supervise their management team in the correct way. Forest chief executive, Phil Soar, responded to the inquiry by announcing: 'The charges referred to all occurred long before the take-over of the club by Nottingham Forest plc and before any directors of the plc were associated with the club. It is our intention to vigorously defend any charges.'

The Inland Revenue were alerted to Alan Sugar's comments in the high court and decided to set up a 'crack team' to investigate any financial irregularities. And they did, getting their teeth into the game and clinging on until they found what they were looking for. They discovered cash payments of tens of thousands of pounds paid to the club for undertaking overseas tours. Transfer fees for players were split between selling clubs and the players. There were 'some cash payments' that were made into numbered bank accounts in Guernsey, probably disguised signing-on fees.

Tax-free *ex gratia* payments were made to some players when they were transferred from Forest and thousands of complimentary tickets for home games were freely distributed to players. In one year, 1989, 20,000 tickets worth £170,000 were given to Forest staff. Routine PAYE and National Insurance payments had not been properly declared.

The Revenue's probe ended in May 1996 with a demand for a payment of £475,000 sent to Forest in respect of undeclared tax. The club were also hit with a £300,000 VAT bill but the combined payments were far less than they had first feared. Despite the serious findings and allegations, Forest got away relatively unscathed. 'The club have adopted the hush-hush approach,' said a senior club insider. 'When people tried to get to the bottom of a number of things they were told to shut up by other members of the board. If anyone ever criticised Brian Clough, or questioned any of his deals, they were sent to Coventry for months on end. It didn't pay to ask too many questions.'

The Revenue forced Brian Clough to pay £600,000 in back tax after he reached a secret settlement with tax inspectors. The four-year probe examined Clough's involvement in at least 58 transfers between April 1987 and April 1993. At the time of the investigation's conclusion, a close associate of Clough said, 'Brian recently told me that the Revenue forced him to pay back £600,000. He just came out with it one day, in a very matter-of-fact fashion. He even joked about it – but deep down I could see that he was glad that all the probing and digging was over. It's taken a terrible toll on him.'

Today, Clough has retired from the game and is a shadow of his former self, suffering poor health and to a point a sullied reputation. He has still not launched legal action against any of his accusers although vigorously denies any wrongdoing himself.

It's rare for internal feuds within football clubs to surface in the public domain but it happened in October 1997 when Middlesbrough's Republic of Ireland defender Curtis Fleming spoke in the press of his fights with Fabrizio Ravanelli. The Italian was not popular with his team-mates: he was aloof, rarely socialised and was forever returning to Italy. Manager Bryan Robson famously joked, 'Ravanelli is really good in the air . . . between England and Italy!' But it wasn't so much his homesickness but his condescending attitude that annoyed his colleagues. Fleming admitted having two punch-ups with Ravanelli before he left Middlesbrough for Olympique Marseille. 'I had a scrap with him at the end of the last season and at the start of this one,' said Fleming. 'People who know me know that I'm not the most aggressive person in the world. It takes a lot to get me going – but I think he knew where he stood with me after that. He's gone now, and it's a good thing. He was never with us. He never came out with us, but we read in the papers that we should be eating this or drinking that, though he never said that to our faces. He got a lot of bad feeling in the club because of the way he did things.'

One of Ravanelli's team-mates also made unsavoury national newspaper headlines over a bust-up with his wife. Craig Hignett was accused by his wife Joely of giving her a black eye during an argument at their family home. Police were called to the house in Inngleby Barwick, Cleveland, but Hignett's wife (a karate expert in her own right) declined to press charges. The following day, however, she returned to the police to make a statement. A Cleveland police spokesman confirmed the news, saying: 'We have received a complaint from Mrs Joely Hignett that she was assaulted by her husband. We are investigating the allegation and he will be questioned as a matter of routine.'

Hignett was quick to jump to his own defence and deny the allegation. 'I am not a wife beater. I have never, ever laid a finger on her, nor would I. If she is saying I have hit her she is lying. And if she has an injury, I had nothing to do with it.' The alleged row between the two had been over Hignett's supposed liaison with local radio presenter Judie McCourt. Hignett denied anything untoward, as did McCourt, who lived on the same upmarket estate as the player. 'I have always said there was nothing going on between Craig and myself and I don't want to make another comment,' she told the *Daily Mirror* on 10 March 1998.

Hignett and his wife Joely were left to sort out their differences with Joely's mother, Dot Tilly, insisting that her daughter was now looking for a divorce. 'Like me she has a black belt in karate,' said Dot. 'She could have laid him out if the children had not been in the house. She wants to name

Judie in divorce papers but the pair of them insist there was nothing going on.'

A man worthy of many a headline, Vinnie Jones has had a colourful career climbing from relative obscurity to national notoriety. He's had as many clubs as you would find in a generous half set in Nick Faldo's garage and has never been far away from controversy. Boisterous to the point of annoying, he has often not been given the credit he deserves for his performances on the pitch. Jones is one of those players who makes good newspaper copy for all the wrong reasons. From hod carrier to Hertfordshire country squire, Jones's most notorious off-field incident was the removal of part of a journalist's nose in a Dublin hotel after England's ill-fated friendly at Landsdowne Road. He bit the journalist and provoked outrage, particularly in view of what had happened at the stadium. The match had been abandoned due to English right-wing football hooligans rearranging the upper level seating in the stand.

In November 1997, Jones was held overnight in a police cell after he allegedly attacked a neighbour. He was accused of smashing his way into Tim Gear's home and assaulting him while he slept. Gear's mother Gillian told the *Sun*, 'Tim was fast asleep in his mobile home when he was suddenly attacked by a man trying to kick and punch it down. He was hit with a hail of punches and kicked all over the body. You only have to look at the boot and fist marks in his home to get an idea of the ferocity.'

Vinnie Jones was arrested and spent the night at St Albans Police Station, charged with criminal assault and damage. His solicitor was at pains to set the record straight. 'Vinnie Jones strenuously denies the charge,' he announced. On his release, Jones declined to comment to waiting reporters.

It emerged that Jones had last spoken to Gear some days before the attack over a dispute where Jones had erected a gate across a path. The Gears pointed out to Vinnie Jones that the path was a public right of way. They asked Jones for a key so that they could get through the gate into the lane and he obliged within a couple of hours.

Police investigating the attack also confiscated shotguns found at Jones's farm. A Hertfordshire police spokesman said: 'It is normal procedure to seize weapons in circumstances such as these. He is a shotgun certificates holder and that will be reviewed in the light of what has happened.'

Jones was bailed to appear at St Alban's Magistrates Court on 18 December 1997 and at the time of writing still has not appeared in court to answer the charges. The legal wrangling goes on but he continues to play football, having moved from Wimbledon to Queens Park Rangers, where he is player-coach.

England captain Alan Shearer, the man who inherited the Golden Boy of English Football title from Gary Lineker, found himself embroiled in newspaper controversy early in 1998. Shearer and his Newcastle United colleagues had flown to Dublin for a spot of rest and recreation straight after a Premier League game, and the papers reported that Shearer and Keith Gillespie were involved in a row that ended in fisticuffs. The England captain was alleged to have been involved in some 'boozy horseplay' in a Dublin bar and argued with Gillespie over the winger's provision of decent crosses for Shearer to score goals from. Phil Norton, a witness to the incident, claimed, 'I saw Shearer get hold of Gillespie by the collar. It looked like Gillespie had had a lot to drink. Shearer pushed him with his right hand and clocked him with the other.'

Shearer, unsurprisingly, was extremely reluctant to talk about the incident and claimed that Gillespie had just slipped. This version of events was fortunately backed up by Newcastle's assistant manager, Terry McDermott (Kenny Dalglish was not in Ireland), despite the fact that he was not present in the bar at the time of the incident. 'On the way out of the bar, Keith tripped and fell. It was decided it was best to go to casualty for a check-up. There was no-one else involved,' said McDermott.

Gillespie was carted off to Meath Hospital where he was given six stitches to a head wound and kept in for 24 hours. Once released, he returned to Newcastle ahead of the rest of the squad. 'I can't remember a thing. I feel fine,' said Gillespie. Upon his return to the north-east, Gillespie kept a low profile until he was arrested and released on police bail pending further enquiries into an alleged incident at a Gateshead hotel on 15 February 1998. For Shearer and his clean-cut image, the whole incident was undoubtedly a worry. However, it's more than likely that the truth will never come out. Footballers are adept at closing ranks when they have to.

No amount of distortions of the truth could save Bayer Leverkusen's striker Ulf Kirsten, who was banned from football for nine weeks in late 1997 for smashing an opponent's face in with his elbow. He was also fined £2,500. Twenty-five-year-old Eamon McHugh was banned from playing anywhere in the world for life for kicking another player in the face. McHugh broke Darren Smith's eye socket, jaw and cheek in a sickening incident and was jailed for three years for the attack in a Barton v. Great Milton match. David Howard of the Oxford Football Association said, 'He will never play again. It is the only way to deal with these people.'

Attacking anyone at a football match is a serious offence but attacking an official is unforgiveable. Thankfully, compared with some countries in the world, this is a rarity in Britain. On 31 January 1998, an unusual incident occurred when John Corker, a Sheffield United fan, attacked linesman Edward Martin at Fratton Park in Portsmouth.

Corker ran on to the pitch and punched Martin after United goalkeeper Simon Tracey was sent off. Referee Mark Halsey had asked Martin his opinion on whether Tracey fouled Portsmouth midfielder Sammy Igoe and when Portsmouth prepared to take the resulting free kick, Martin slumped to the ground about two yards inside the pitch. Referee Halsey said, 'I was totally numbed by the attack. I've never seen anything like it in all my years in football.

'I saw the man running along the touchline and throw a punch, but there was nothing I could do to stop him. It was frightening.'

Edward Martin himself remembers very little of the attack: 'I was aware of some unrest in the crowd behind me after the Sheffield United goalkeeper was sent off. The referee came over to ask my opinion. I saw the referee show the red card and the keeper take off his jersey. After that, it's a blank. The next thing I knew was waking up on a stretcher and being taken to an ambulance,' he said.

Martin spent a night in Portsmouth's Queen Alexandra Hospital. The FA launched an inquiry into the incident while other interested parties speculated over a return to perimeter fencing, a suggestion that was swiftly rebuked by the football authorities. Both team managers condemned the attack with Portsmouth's Alan Ball saying, 'It was one of the worst scenes that I've witnessed. You hear about it happening in places like Uruguay and Chile but not here. This yob should never see another football match in his life. They should even black out his TV.'

Sheffield United's manager, Nigel Spackman, agreed with Ball, adding, 'We can just hope the football authorities and the police make sure he never attends another football match in his life.'

Corker was found guilty of assault with actual bodily harm by Portsmouth magistrates and Sheffield United banned him from attending any matches at Bramall Lane for life.

If these are relatively isolated incidents in the British game, the same cannot be said about our near neighbours on the Continent. Football violence is on the increase across the whole of continental Europe, from Spain to Germany, France to Holland – and none more so than in Italy. 'Ultras' are a group of football thugs who follow a number of Italian clubs. Their currency is frightening violence, drugs trafficking and fighting with each other and the police. They are racist too – at Verona, in Serie 'B', home Ultras vehemently protested at their club signing the black Dutch international, Ferrer, and hoisted a cardboard black figure in a Verona kit being hung on the gallows. Understandably, Ferrer decided to cancel his transfer without further ado. The Ultras thrive on stadium violence and in February 1998 Verona and Salerno Ultras clashed, forcing the game to be stopped for several minutes until police brought them under control by using tear gas. Incensed by a series of poor results, Genoa Ultras, armed with baseball bats, vaulted the fence of their club's training ground and attacked the players while they were playing a mid-week practice match. The players sprinted for cover but two of them ended up on the club's long-term injury list.

That's not all. A fan was stabbed to death by Milan Ultras

outside Genoa's stadium and, for the first time in Italian sporting history, all sports fixtures were suspended throughout the country the following weekend as a mark of respect and a show of solidarity against violence at football matches. A Lazio fan was accidentally killed during the Roma–Lazio derby when he was hit by a flare fired by the Roma Ultras. Italian politicians have been appalled and embarrassed by the behaviour, prompting one to announce, 'We need English-style stadiums and security.' An irony if ever there was one.

As football becomes increasingly popular so does the intensity of the media's scrutiny of the game. Gone are the days of rich benefactors solely controlling clubs. Today the plc is king. Clubs floated on the market have to answer to their shareholders and the city suits and money men who are becoming football's powerbrokers. Many fans feel detached from their clubs and suspicious of their motives. However, despite all the fancy wheeling and dealing, the supporters remain the lifeblood of a club, and chairmen and boards ignore and abuse them at their peril.

Never in the history of English football has the fan/board of directors relationship been called into question in such a public way than when Newcastle United's chairman Freddy Shepherd and vice-chairman Doug Hall were splashed all over the front of the *News of the World* in March 1998. The pair, said the paper, had been caught by an undercover reporter in a Spanish brothel.

Hall and Shepherd had flown to Spain to meet with some businessmen from Dubai whom, they were told, were keen to expand football in the Emirate and even put in a late bid for the 2006 World Cup finals. The Newcastle pair had been celebrating Newcastle's FA Cup quarter-final win over

Barnsley with a considerable amount of drink, which they freely admit. Over glasses of champagne, they told one of the businessmen that Newcastle had sold Andy Cole to Manchester United in the knowledge that he had a career-threatening injury. Gullible fans, they laughed, paid up to £50 for replica shirts that were made in Asia at a cost of £5. The two talked about travelling the world paying for sex, said the newspaper. Shepherd explained that this was a necessity because, 'Newcastle girls are all dogs. England is full of them. The girls are ugly and they're dogs. We've had *Penthouse* pets, the fucking lot. The best in the world.' Douglas Hall chipped in, claiming to have had 'six hundred, seven hundred mistresses.'

The three men moved on from the hotel bar to an upmarket brothel called Milady Palace, where Shepherd allegedly demanded a lesbian show with handcuffs. As the conversation continued, over more drinks, Freddy Shepherd mocked some of the club's personalities. He said of former manager Kevin Keegan: 'We used to call him Shirley Temple. We sacked him because we gave him £60 million to spend and we won nothing.' They then went on to discuss the problems with Alan Shearer, Newcastle's star player. 'He's boring,' said Shepherd. 'We call him Mary Poppins. He never gets into trouble.'

The *News of the World* never accused the men of having sex with prostitutes but the ramblings of Hall and Shepherd left people in no doubt as to what they thought of the world's oldest profession. Having moved on to another bar, The Crescendo, on Puerto Banus, they decided to list their favourite brothels and prostitutes. 'Geneva – that's the best for girls. Thousands of beautiful girls – Russian, Chinese, Japanese, American, French, Swedish, English,' said Hall.

'Le Mans. When we had the car race in France we had a Serb, two Poles, two French, two Russians and a Chinese (prostitute, not takeaway!). We took our football team and we couldn't believe it. We had the army guarding us. We went into a nightclub and the army threw everybody out, grabbed hold of every girl and said, "Sit there." We were sat there going, "This is good." '

The revelations of Shepherd and Hall infuriated supporters of Newcastle United and journalists had a field day. City concerns were in tandem with those of the supporters. John Regan, secretary of the Independent Newcastle United Supporters' Association, said, 'This has to be a resigning matter. They will both have to go and they must go quickly.'

Newcastle legend Malcolm Macdonald agreed. 'They have to resign. This despicable pair have disgraced and insulted the Geordie nation. They have destroyed the reputation of one of the greatest clubs in the world. How can they sit in the stand for the next game just yards from the people they ridiculed?'

The situation quickly became a free for all. Adidas dismissed claims that the Asian-made replica shirts cost £5. 'They are made in the UK and cost considerably more,' said a spokesman.

The fans remained furious and, following Newcastle's 2-1 home defeat to Crystal Palace, called for Hall and Shepherd's resignation. Such was the pressure on Newcastle's board that three other members threatened to resign if Hall and Shepherd did not leave. One of them, Sir Terence Harrison, chairman of engineering giants Alfred McAlpine, said, 'We are considering our position, yes. That's all I'm prepared to say.'

A week after its initial revelations, the *News of the World* printed more information which made even more uncomfortable reading for the club and the supporters. Freddy Shepherd tried unsuccessfully at the high court to prevent the further newspaper allegations from reaching the public domain. Mr Justice Lindsay said, 'Shepherd and Hall made a long series of boastful, lewd statements bragging about the way they whored their way around the world. If they were in and out of brothels in all the places mentioned, can they expect behaviour of that type to remain in confidence?'

The *News of the World* quoted Shepherd as saying, 'We like our fans to get drunk because we own the bars where they drink, so we can't complain too much about drunken behaviour.'

Other comments included Douglas Hall's confident 'Forget Paul Gascoigne. He's finished,' and Shepherd's dismissive 'Albert, he's nearly finished. Probably two more years left in football.' Gary Lineker was written off as a potential manager as he was a waste of time who speaks on television and does adverts for crisps, said the pair.

On Monday 23 March 1998, sports minister Tony Banks branded Hall and Shepherd 'despicable loudmouths unfit to run a public company. Their conduct has brought their club and the game of soccer into disrepute. They should go – and go fast. Fans' money is being used to pay for private jets, boozing and loose women. Even if they go, it will be with pockets stuffed with money – a huge pot of gold filled by loyal fans.'

The *Sun* ran a story the same day, reporting that Hall had allegedly thrown a party at his father's home, Wynyard Hall, for 40 friends featuring topless waitresses, strippers, mud wrestlers and a four-girl lesbian show. His parents were out of the country at the time of the party.

Shepherd and Hall received some unlikely backing when former manager Kevin Keegan spoke about the tremendous work the two had done for Newcastle United over the years and Mary Poppins, aka Alan Shearer, chipped in to say that no-one was a bigger Newcastle United fanatic than Hall or Shepherd. Nevertheless, the pair resigned late that evening, issuing a statement which said: 'Douglas Hall and Freddy Shepherd have decided to step down as directors of Newcastle plc and Newcastle Football Company. They arrived at the decision in order to ensure that the allegations made against them do not further affect Newcastle United and to enable them to concentrate their energies in restoring their reputations. Nothing that has happened in the past week diminishes their dedication to the success of Newcastle United.'

Former chairman Sir John Hall agreed to take over until the end of the season and at an emotional press conference defended his son and Shepherd, insisting that they had been set up. According to the *Guardian*, he may have had a case. Sir John Hall used the phrase 'elaborate and expensive scam' and pointed the finger firmly at the *News of the World*. Editor Phil Hall (no relation!) said, 'The people we are exposing always try to shoot the messenger. They always say, "They set us up." ' As far as he was concerned, the resignation of Shepherd and Hall vindicated his paper's investigations. The *Guardian*, however, reported that far from being a simple investigation, it was a sophisticated sting operation in which an odd assortment of characters played leading roles. The story was credited to Mazher Mahmood, investigations editor – a man whose undercover work the SAS would envy – and three other participants. The *Guardian* claimed that a 'foreign emissary' made several telephone calls to Newcastle, asking if the club could help Dubai to be put on the footballing map. The club believed this could be an excellent opportunity so a go-between arrived, calling himself John Hiller (in reality John Miller). He was checked out and considered sincere and it was agreed that Hall and Shepherd would travel to Marbella to meet Hiller's bosses.

At the hotel, the pair claim that they were offered champagne from a bottle which was already open – significant, as Hall and Shepherd believe the drink was spiked. One witness in Spain was quoted as saying that Douglas Hall 'talked like a machine gun' – a claim that surprised Hall's friends as he has a reputation for being a man of few words. They were introduced to the Arabs, with Mahmood and another man also present, dressed in traditional robes and headdresses. The famous interview then continued but, according to the *Guardian*, the key to understanding why they said what they said lies in the context. They were a couple of businessmen doing business; talking up their own importance, boasting about probable profits and when referring to sex, saying what they imagined Middle Eastern men would like to hear. The *Guardian*'s Roy Greenslade wondered whether some of the more offensive quotes about women were discussed in the context of prostitutes. Although still grossly offensive, if this theory is right, it does place the matter in a different light.

Undercover reporter Mahmood was accompanied by a second 'Arab' whom the *Mirror* named as Paul Samrai – a man jailed for three years in 1993 for a £1 million racket involving the sale of forged passports in Hong Kong. (The *News of the World*, however, were adamant that he did not take part.)

Go-between John Miller also has an unsavoury past. Among his exploits was the kidnapping of the Great Train Robber, Ronnie Biggs, in 1981. He often 'helped' in some of the *News of the World*'s seamier stories through his friendship with one of the paper's former reporters, Gerry Brown, who wrote a book about investigative journalism called *Exposed*. The Hall/Shepherd story certainly bore the hallmarks of the kind of operation described in the book.

If, as Greenslade suggests, Mahmood and his team acted as *agents provocateurs*, it opens up a series of interesting questions. Why did the *News of the World* target these men? Who tipped them off and why? They weren't breaking any laws, so what did the paper hope to discover?

The *News of the World* could argue that two rich men drinking excessively and bragging about their sexual conquests is a legitimate story in the public interest. Hall and Shepherd were directors of a public company and without a doubt behaved badly, but did they behave any differently to any other businessmen or Newcastle fans put in similar circumstances?

Self-regulation is expected of players, and referees do the job for them if they stray off the straight and narrow. In March 1998, however, a Sunday League referee, Martin Sylvester, sent himself off after attacking a player. The incident happened during a 2-2 draw between the Southampton Arms and Hurstbourne Tarrant British Legion in the Andover and District Sunday League. Sylvester was the manager of the Southampton Arms team and only stepped in to take charge when the original official fell ill. Sylvester had refereed over 40 games in two years and explained, 'I was sorely provoked. I punched him several times after he pushed me from behind. He then swore. I just couldn't take any more – I blew my top. Everyone dived in to pull me off him. But I should not have done it. It was bad behaviour by me. Now I am not going to get involved in football any more. I have blown my whistle for the last time.'

The punched player, Richard Curd, 27, said, 'The ref gave me a black eye when he punched me. He hit me several times in the face and head. I deny ever pushing him or provoking him. We collided with each other accidentally as I was chasing after the ball.' Sylvester was the subject of a top-level inquiry by the Andover and District Sunday League.

Even club mascots have landed themselves in hot water. In March 1998, Aston Villa sacked their mascot, Hercules the Lion, after he 'mauled' a beauty queen on the pitch. The lion, alias Gavin Lucas, grabbed Miss Aston Villa, Debbie Robins, and kissed her during the half-time interval of the match between Villa and Crystal Palace. Lucas defended himself after the incident: 'It was just a bit of fun. What's the world coming to if you can't play around with someone? There was nothing sexual in it. I just gave Debbie a sort of grapple, a bear hug, grabbing her waist with my paws and pulling her around. I gave her a kiss too but it wasn't much of one because I had my lion's head on. I tried to explain that I didn't mean anything by it but it was caught on camera and shown on screens around the ground and the club decided it was unprofessional. Now I know what it feels like for a manager to be sacked. I'm gutted but I'll never stop supporting Villa.'

David Ismay, Villa's head of projects, offered the club's view. 'Gavin just gets a bit carried away. Perhaps it's the heat inside the lion's suit but he does let his heart rule his head sometimes.'

It emerged that Lucas had already received an official warning from Aston Villa after parading in front of Coventry fans, kissing the badge on his Villa shirt.

Bolton mascot, Lofty the Lion, went one better and was sacked in 1997 for making rude gestures at Wolverhampton Wanderers supporters and pelting them with meat pies!

2 Africa

F EUROPE IS THE GRANDFATHER of football, then Africa is the grandson, a continent so rich and varied in culture that it has struggled to achieve a cohesive football development. The 1990s have been a period of great change in African football, with less reliance on foreign coaches and more belief in the way forward on a homegrown level. Things could be about to change as the African nations tap into their abundant natural resources – the players.

In 1962, England manager Walter Winterbottom boldly predicted that an African nation would win the World Cup. Of course, his prediction did not come true, as Morocco were knocked out by Spain in the third qualifying round and Ethiopia lost 4-2 on aggregate to Israel. Indeed, world football is still waiting for its first African World Cup winners but, law of averages aside, that significant day may not be so far away.

Politics is almost as important as tactics in African football. Egypt became the first African nation to reach the World Cup finals in 1934. To qualify they beat Palestine 11-2 on aggregate but, in the tournament proper, lost 4-2 to Hungary in the first round. The Egyptians declined the chance to play in the 1938 finals by refusing to play

Romania in a qualifying match. In 1958, temperamental problems once again hampered the Egyptians' assault on the greatest prize in world football. They reached the second qualifying round but then withdrew, allowing their intended opponents Sudan to go through to the third qualifying round. Sudan were drawn against Israel and also pulled out in a political protest over the newly formed Jewish state.

African nations decided to boycott the 1966 finals in England on account of the fact that FIFA awarded the continent only a play-off for a place in the finals against the best Asian team. It took until the qualifying stages for the 1970 finals in Mexico before FIFA finally gave Africa its own qualifying competition – but only eleven countries bothered to enter. Bizarrely, Morocco qualified for the finals after a lucky coin toss with Tunisia and went on to frighten the lives out of the West Germans by taking an early 1-0 lead, only to finally succumb to two German goals. Morocco did achieve Africa's first point in the World Cup finals by drawing with Bulgaria.

The next World Cup, in 1974, was a significant year for the continent when Zaire became the first black African nation to qualify for the finals. The media showed their fascination by stating that the players' pre-tournament diet included monkey. Zaire's Yugoslav coach, Blagoyev Vidinic, decided to remove his goalkeeper after conceding a third goal against Yugoslavia, and when asked after the match for his reasoning behind the substitution, he claimed he was only doing what the Zaire sports minister had asked him to do. Zaire lost the match 9-0 and Vidinic was accused of being a Yugoslav agent. A little strong, perhaps – sympathiser would have been more appropriate.

Four years later, in 1978, Zaire pulled out of the World

Cup claiming that some of their players were behaving unpatriotically. Tunisia were left to fly the African flag in impressive style, drawing 0-0 with West Germany and inflicting a 3-1 defeat on Mexico, only exiting the tournament on goal difference to Poland.

Two African nations qualified for the 1982 finals in Spain. Cameroon drew 1-1 with Italy (who went on to win the tournament) and eventually went out on goal difference. Algeria thoroughly deserved a second-round place after wins over West Germany (1-0) and Chile (3-2) but FIFA's scheduling allowed West Germany and Austria to play out a farcical 1-0 win for the Germans, which saw both countries go through at Algeria's expense. The match became known as the 'Great Gijon Swindle' and was clearly fixed – although FIFA chose not to investigate.

1990 was the year that the bungling Sengalese forgot to enter the World Cup qualification round and saw the emergence of Egypt and Cameroon as significant football powers. Egypt went out in the group stages while Cameroon defeated defending world champions Argentina 1-0 in the opening match despite being down to nine men. What the Lions of Cameroon lacked in tactical and tackling skills, they more than made up for with their fast, flowing, skilful football. Roger Milla became one of the stars of the tournament and his goals helped Cameroon become the first African nation to reach the quarter-finals of a World Cup. Only their inability to not give away penalties to England led to an earlier World Cup exit than they perhaps deserved. Despite their sometimes naive spells in matches, Cameroon had confirmed that African football was becoming a force to be reckoned with on the international stage – but still journalists insisted on asking questions on anything but their performance on the pitch. Francios Oman Bayik complained that the first question he was asked by the world's media was whether the Cameroon team burned chickens before a match.

Nigeria's emergence as a significant footballing nation culminated in their qualification for the 1994 finals in America with Dutch coach Clemens Westerhof. Nigeria faced Italy in the second round of USA 94 and showed little respect, claiming in the pre-match 'mind games' press conferences that 'Italy is famous for the Mafia and Fiat, not football'. On the pitch, Nigeria came within two minutes of sending the Italians home. Roberto Baggio grabbed an equaliser and the Italians went through and progressed to the final, only to be beaten on penalties by Brazil.

Cameroon, meanwhile, had started the tournament in disarray, refusing to play their opening match against Brazil unless they got paid. Reports claimed that a suitcase containing $450,000 was flown over from the Cameroon capital, Yaounde. It was to no avail, however, as they lost 3-0 to Brazil and 6-1 to Russia.

The new 32-nation World Cup finals in France saw the most amount of African qualifiers – Nigeria, Tunisia, South Africa, Cameroon and Morocco. The confidence of the Nigerians seems to have rubbed off on a large section of Africa's football journalists. One leading writer is convinced – 'If Nigeria don't win, it will be because everyone's been plotting against them.'

Yet, as African football has developed, so too has its capacity for dodgy dealings. The Nigerian FA excelled themselves in unsavoury behaviour when they decided to team up with Dutchman Clemens Westerhof in 1989. Westerhof was handed the job of technical adviser to the Nigerian national team, after a stint as caretaker coach at Feyenoord in Rotterdam. He held the post until just after the

1994 World Cup finals in America, almost certainly failing to realise what he had got himself into from the start. He accepted the job in mid 1989 when Nigeria were striving to qualify for the 1990 World Cup in Italy but his credentials were questioned by some sections of the Nigerian media who felt (rightly or wrongly) that Westerhof's football track record was not quite what was required by an emerging international football team.

Prior to Westerhof's arrival, Paul Hamilton had been Nigeria's coach. Not one person from the Nigerian FA had remotely hinted that he was about to be replaced. In a less than subtle move, the Nigerian FA invited Westerhof to the Gabonese capital, Libreville, to watch Nigeria play a World Cup qualifying tie against the Azingo Nationale (Gabon). Hamilton got wind of Westerhof's visit through some of his allies in the Nigerian FA, and naturally his appetite for the match was somewhat diminished. So much so that he provided no assistance to the team and Nigeria were beaten 2-1. By biting the hand that fed them, the Nigerian FA had ensured that qualification for the World Cup was an impossibility.

Westerhof was duly installed as coach and faced his first major test when Nigeria played Cameroon at the Stade D'Omnisport in Yaounde, in their final World Cup qualification game. It was an encounter in which Nigeria were destined to fail.

Things didn't start well. Midfielder Etim Esin refused to board the plane at Murtala Mohammed Airport in Lagos, stating that he required a cash payment of $5,000 before he would agree to play for Nigeria. The reason for the cash request was simple: Esin suspected that some of his team-mates were being given large appearance fees and naturally he wanted a piece of the action.

Richard Owubokiri, a top star with Benfica, insisted that his Brazilian wife should be allowed to accompany the team for the trip to Cameroon or he would refuse to play. Clemens Westerhof then dropped goalkeeper Peter Rufai, generally acknowledged as one of Africa's top keepers and certainly the Nigerian No. 1. Westerhof's lack of knowledge where African football was concerned was extremely worrying, but he insisted that all was OK – his demoted assistant manager, Paul Hamilton, had recommended the move and kindly provided him with an accurate dossier on the Cameroon players.

Following the match, Westerhof told Godwin Dudu Orumen, one of Nigeria's leading football pundits, that Hamilton must have deliberately given him incorrect information on the Cameroon team, rendering Nigeria's tactics wholly ineffectual. Hamilton himself clearly hoped that the outcry following a Nigerian defeat would be enough to earn Westerhof the sack and reinstate him as team coach. It was not to be.

Westerhof had also been told by Hamilton that Emmanuel Kunde – arguably the best African central defender at the time – was an attacker. Feeling betrayed, from that time forward the new coach decided never to have complete trust in any Nigerian football coach again. Indeed, he quickly realised that he would need cunning, guile, diplomacy and a ruthless streak with Nigerian FA officials if he was to always be one step ahead during his time in the job.

After his failure to lead Nigeria to the 1990 World Cup finals, Westerhof's next major challenge was to win the 1990 African Nations Cup in Algeria. Several top players refused to play for Nigeria (Stephen Keshi and Samson Siasia among them) so Westerhof was forced to field a largely inexperienced team. One such player was seventeen-year-old

Daniel Amokachi, who was the youngest player ever to take part in the African Nations Cup. In the opening game, Nigeria were thrashed 5-1 by hosts Algeria. The Nigerian media's knives were sharpened and Westerhof's reign as coach looked to be short lived. Miraculously, he turned things round and, with a mixture of good fortune and flowing football, reached the final only to be beaten 1-0.

While the Nigerian public tolerated Westerhof, he had many critics. Arrogance was one of the major complaints about this *modus operandi* but nobody could deny that he was a survivor. Boldly, Westerhof stated that Nigeria would win the 1992 African Nations Cup – and if they didn't, he would resign. It was a promise not driven by history – the last time Nigeria had won the African Nations Cup was in 1980 when they were the host nation.

In the event, Nigeria lost in the semi-finals to Ghana and despite his word, Westerhof refused to resign. He did claim to have sent a letter of resignation to Alex Akinyele, executive chairman of Nigeria's National Sports Commission, who then 'prevailed upon' him to withdraw it.

Whatever the truth, a major confrontation between the two men took place during the last game of the World Cup 94 African-zone qualifiers between Nigeria and Algeria in Algiers. Despite managing to score a vital away goal, giving Nigeria a 1-0 lead at half time, Westerhof was stunned when Akinyele marched into the dressing room and berated the players. It was an incident that he never forgot. 'He came into our dressing room at half time on the pretext of giving the boys a pep talk. But instead of commending the players for scoring a crucial away goal he said that my players were playing like pregnant women. Can you imagine that? They were 45 minutes away from making their debut appearance at the World Cup finals!'

Westerhof was furious and asked Akinyele if he had finished delivering his 'words of encouragement' to the players. Having said enough, Akinyele stalked out of the dressing room, only to almost have his head taken off as Westerhof slammed the door after him. Nigeria won the match and qualified for the finals but the celebrations were significantly dampened because of the dressing room bust-up. On the return flight to Lagos, Akinyele refused to join in the victory celebrations because he felt humiliated by Westerhof's actions.

Alex Akinyele was generally regarded as more of a clown than a sports minister and was sacked by Nigeria's military dictator, Sani Abacha, soon after. Westerhof, presuming his job was safe, looked forward to the future with optimism. He was brought very quickly down to earth when Abacha informed him that failure to win the 1994 African Nations Cup in Tunisia would lead to his sacking and so end his involvement in Nigeria's forthcoming World Cup campaign.

To his credit, Westerhof managed to deliver what the Nigerians had been craving – the 1994 African Nations Cup – but not without a lot of blood, sweat and tears. During the campaign, Westerhof had many battles with Samson Omeruah, chairman of the Nigerian FA, and his assistant Jo Bonfrere, over team selection matters. One of the major sources of disagreement was the use of left winger Emmanuel Amunike (previous clubs Sporting Lisbon and Barcelona). Bonfrere was adamant that he deserved a place in the first team but Westerhof disagreed. In fact, Westerhof flatly refused to play him in the tournament but, succumbing to intimidating pressure, picked him for the final against Zambia.

Amunike proved to be a rather valuable addition to the

team, scoring both goals in a memorable victory for Nigeria. Rather than confess to the media that he never had any intention of playing Amunike, Westerhof insisted that he had 'reserved' Amunike as a secret weapon, a claim which was met with scorn.

In the months leading up to the 1994 World Cup in the United States, Sylvanus Akinwunmi was appointed as the sports minister. He was known to be a great admirer of English coaches and liked the idea of an English manager taking over from Westerhof before the finals. Discreet and covert approaches were made to Terry Venables but nothing came of it. A worried Clemens Westerhof rallied his allies in the Nigerian FA and managed to hang on to his job. Such was his ability to manipulate his way through Nigerian football officialdom that he earned the nickname 'Dutch-gerian'.

Westerhof did not always enjoy the respect of his players, some of whom accused him of personally selling Nigerian players to several top European clubs, which was regarded as unethical because he was the national coach.

It became increasingly apparent that Westerhof's footballing ambitions didn't just lie on the pitch, and his 'agency' work began taking up valuable time and possibly affected his judgement. Victor Ikpeba, the 1997 African Footballer of the Year (he plays as a striker for Monaco), accuses Westerhof of refusing to field players who wouldn't come under his personal management. 'Westerhof never liked me because he could not sell me to any European club. He did go as far as trying to remove my name from the list of 22 players that had been sent to FIFA for the World Cup finals in the USA, because some officials from the Nigerian FA put pressure on him to pick players from the northern part of the country. Pressure was put on me to tell

FIFA that I was injured so that they could substitute my name with that of Tijani Babangida (of Ajax Amersterdam) but I bluntly refused to do this because I felt that this was an act of injustice that was being committed against me.'

Peter Rufai, goalkeeper with the Nigerian team, added credence to the allegations when he appeared on Dutch national television in 1993 declaring that 'Westerhof is a fake', having made close to a million dollars selling Nigerian players in Europe. When the Nederlandse Omroepp Stiching (Dutch TV) invited Westerhof to reply to the charges, he apparently declined the chance to respond for reasons best known to himself.

Westerhof's activities caused friction between German Bundesliga side MSV Duisburg and Sporting Lisbon, who were both vying for the services of Emmanuel Amunike after the 1994 World Cup. After distinguishing himself as a star player in the Egyptian League with Zamalek, Amunike's impressive performances at the 1994 World Cup made him hot property in Europe but, by his own admission, the player had put himself in a quandary. Amunike said that under intimidation from Clemens Westerhof, who told him that he would not go to the World Cup unless he let him become his agent, Amunike signed a contractual agreement, allegedly under duress, agreeing to make his debut for MSV Duisburg after the World Cup. However, Amunike preferred a lucrative offer from Sporting Lisbon and made it clear that he was going to sign a contract in spite of the agreement he had entered into with MSV Duisburg. In an interview with an African soccer magazine, Westerhof denied any involvement with the contractual mess, saying, 'The statements that Emmanuel made are lies and he knows it. He said the same things in a television interview but claimed that it was one of my assistants. He has to learn to keep his mouth shut. I'm now looking at the affair with my lawyers and if I can take it to court then I will.' He never did.

FIFA intervened and directed that Sporting Lisbon should pay MSV Duisburg $1.4 million if they wanted Amunike's transfer to go ahead.

During the 1994 World Cup, Westerhof faced a players' mutiny before Nigeria's second-round match against Italy in Boston, Massachusetts. The players were under a strict sex ban at the team hotel but several decided to sneak their girlfriends in at odd hours of the day and night. Westerhof found out and moved the players to another hotel. They rebelled against the decision and the situation deteriorated. Westerhof recalls: 'Before the Italy match, I saw the players had lost concentration, so I suggested that we move to another hotel. Some of them had their wives with them, and some other ladies came . . . One night, six of the players were out until 6 a.m. I told the Minister of Youth and Sport and the FA chairman that team discipline was slipping and that we had to leave the hotel.

'Everybody agreed and I went with a board member to book into the Sheraton. When we got back the players said that they would not go. Someone from the Nigerian FA board had tipped them off. Instead of accepting that I had brought them this far and that they should take my advice, they refused to move. From that moment we had lost the match with Italy. We didn't lose the match on the pitch but off it.'

Many Nigerian football commentators were highly critical of Westerhof's tactics against the Italians and were at a loss to understand why, early in the match, when Daniel Amokachi and Emmanuel Amunike had to be replaced through injury, the ideal substitutes – Samson Sia Sia and Victor Ikpeba – were not introduced. The reason was simple. Westerhof clashed with both players on a personal level so he vowed not to use them in the World Cup.

Dr Tunde Amao, the Nigerian team doctor, sat next to Westerhof and Jo Bonfrere on the team bench in the pitch-side dug-out and remembers Bonfrere and Westerhof having a furious argument mid match. 'When Westerhof substituted the two attackers for two midfielders, Bonfrere asked him why he did it because he felt that he needed extra fire power up front, as the Italians were already a man down – Chelsea's Gianfranco Zola was sent off – but he decided to ignore his assistant's advice, saying that he had made his decisions and no-one could question it.'

When Nigeria lost the match, Emeka Ezeugo, one of the defenders not used during the tournament, threatened to beat Westerhof into a pulp. The Dutchman took the threat of assault very seriously and fled the team hotel immediately after the match. It was a sad end to Westerhof's tenure as manager of the Nigerian team.

After his five-year stint with Nigeria, Westerhof's next assignment was with Mamelodi Sundowns, in the First Division of South Africa's National Soccer League. However, he was unable to shake off his controversial image and was immersed in trouble once again at an Inisa Charity Cup game between the Sundowns and the Kaiser Chiefs. Westerhof's side lost the match 20-1 and he refused to answer the questions posed by a pint-sized South African journalist. Annoyed with his persistence, Westerhof seized the journalist's microphone and apparently broke it in two pieces. He vehemently denied the attack and claimed the journalist was trading on his reputation and making a mountain out of a molehill. Westerhof said, 'I was having a chat with him and his microphone accidentally dropped.'

All was not well with his players, who resented his authoritarian attitude. Eventually, it became so much of a problem that Mamelodi Sundowns gave him the sack, claiming that they could no longer guarantee his safety and security in South Africa, although the reality was probably that his face didn't fit so he had to go.

African football's problems are continent wide and infiltrate everywhere from the largest to the smallest countries. The Ivory Coast is not the most likely port of call in a roll call of wrongdoing but it has seen its fair share of problems. In 1995, Craven 'A' League champions, Africa Sports, were stripped of their title after it was discovered that one of their players, Bamba Ladji, had lied about his true identity when he applied for a player's licence. Despite having been registered by Ivorian Football Federation supremo Dieng Oussenyou, it was decided that an example should be made of Africa Sports to deter other clubs from signing fictitious players. Not only were they stripped of their title; they were also kicked out of the Ivorian FA Cup at the semi-final stage.

In the early 1990s, Oumar Ben Salah was the Ivory Coast's most influential midfield player. He played for the French club side Le Mans, but in 1993 it was discovered that he and his second wife, Marie Laure, had badly abused their young son, Mohammed. The prosecution evidence revealed that Oumar Ben Salah had been beating his son frequently and, despite her knowledge of his actions, his wife had done nothing to stop the abuse. When the scandal broke in France, the Ivorian authorities knew that his absence from the national side would hinder their progress in the remaining games of the World Cup preliminary matches and would have a significant effect on their long-term World Cup qualification chances. Considerable pressure was put on the French authorities to deal with Ben Salah leniently but to no avail. Ben Salah was not only jailed but stripped of his French citizenship as well. Frank Simon, a journalist with *France Football*, saw the extent of the injuries sustained by Mohammed. 'You need to see the pictures that were taken of Mohammed. They were terrible. You just can't believe that any parent would be capable of that,' he commented.

Controversy and Nigeria seem to go hand in hand, and while the male national team are specialists in erratic and dubious behaviour, the female national team have not been without their problems either. As women's football becomes bigger and bigger around the globe so does the importance of the Women's World Cup. The first tournament of its kind was held in China in 1991. Africa was allocated one qualifying spot and Nigeria were successful in securing it, but not before some local difficulties were sorted out. Nigerian minister of sport, Major General Y. Y. Kure, considered it a complete waste of time and resources. He considered it far more important to support the male national side's quest for the 1992 African Nations Cup. Nevertheless, the Nigerian ladies' team had qualified and Kure was overruled by Mrs Maryam Babangida – wife of Nigeria's erstwhile dictator, Ibrahmi Babangida – who ensured that they took their rightful place at the World Cup.

It was a disaster waiting to happen. Some of the players were exchanging financial favours with top Nigerian FA and Sports Ministry officials for sexual gratification. Pauline Walley, a sports journalist with one of Nigeria's leading dailies, *The National Concord*, suspected that something was amiss when the team's chaperone for the tournament, Lt Chidi Amaechina, a Nigerian naval officer, was mysteriously dropped from the delegation. She had been instrumental in enforcing team discipline among the players throughout qualification, so Pauline Walley decided to keep a close eye on the conduct of the girls in China. Gaining the confidence of certain players, quite a story began to unfold before her. She collated her findings and passed them on to her sports editor, Kunle Solja, whose slight delay in running with the story allowed another Nigerian newspaper, the *Sporting Champion*, to report the facts to the Nigerian public on Friday 22 November, 1991.

Two Nigerian female officials were then approached by a reporter from the *Sporting Champion* but they refused to confirm or deny the cash-for-sex allegations. They did, however, suggest that if the reporter wanted to find out the truth he should contact the male officials who were widely suspected to be the culprits. 'We brought the girls here to play football and they [the men] are defiling them,' they added.

Mr P. O. C. Achebe, who was the head of the Nigerian delegation at the World Cup and assistant coach, Paul Hamilton, furiously denied that any such thing had taken place. Paul Bassey, editor of the *Sporting Champion*, knew better, and in December 1991 wrote an extensive article giving precise details of the sex scandal.

Journalist Pauline Walley went public with what she knew, claiming that six girls (who she refused to name) were the ones who got special 'favours' from a man who was in charge of cash allocation to the girls in China. Sports minister Kure had sent this man with the money that the girls would need but these allowances were then reduced. It soon became evident, however, that the 'favoured six' were still able to get all they wanted in terms of cash. Other team members were jealous that they had not attracted such sexual interest and began to spill the beans. When Pauline Walley confronted the suspects, they refused to confirm or deny the allegations, which 'confirmed my suspicions', said Walley.

In spite of the furore raised in the media, none of the officals suspected in the cash-for-sex scandal received the slightest reprimand from the Nigerian authorities.

In African football folklore, Roger Milla is in a league of his own, and can fill up column inches in newspapers without any trouble. Milla first came to international attention after his breathtaking performances for Cameroon in the 1990 World Cup finals in Italy, and many thought he would be laughing all the way to the bank as a result of a deluge of offers that were sure to come his way. Sadly, it was not to be.

Arguably, Milla is the most famous footballer ever to emerge from African international football, not to mention the most temperamental. In December 1991, he insisted on a massive appearance fee from the English FA to play a friendly game against England at Wembley. Ultimately, he did not play because the standard appearance fee offered to him was not enough.

This tendency for uncompromising demands was a source of great amusement to the Nigerians in 1990. Milla arrived in Lagos to pick up his well-deserved African Player of the Year Award and immediately requested an appearance fee of $10,000 to play in the game that was being staged in his honour – he was due to play 45 minutes for each team. Milla then had a request for Nigerian multi-millionaire Bashorun

MKO Abiola, who was bankrolling the awards. He suggested that Abiola should buy him two coaches so that he could start up his own transport business back home in Cameroon. Not surprisingly, the Nigerians sent him packing with his award and nothing else.

After Italia 90, Milla played most of his football in France, enjoying spells with Bastia, Valenciennes and Montpellier. However, for a player of his talent, there was a commonly held view that Milla did not reap the rewards that his ability warranted. Frank Simon, African football correspondent for *France Football*, says, 'For all his fame, Milla did not get the financial rewards that a player of his status should have received. In most of his contract negotiations he was terribly cheated. As a matter of fact, he was paid peanuts during the most productive part of his football career. As a Frenchman, I feel ashamed that he has been treated this way in my own country.'

Explanation, perhaps, for some of Milla's 'appearance' demands – if only he had thought of engaging Clemens Westerhof as his agent, things could have been much different. Milla's frustration and bitterness at his financial return from his career in football forced him to accept an offer, after the 1994 World Cup finals, to play for Pelita Jaya in the Indonesian League.

Milla is not the only African star who has been taken advantage of by his employers. Nigerian Rashidi Yekini, a huge star in Africa who impressed a worldwide audience at USA 94, ended up top scorer for Vitoria Setubal, the Portuguese First Division side, in the season after the 1994 World Cup. Yekini was transferred to Vitoria Setubal from top Ivory Coast side Africa Sports in 1989, but it emerged that his wages were equivalent to a footballing slave. The initial 1989 contract with Setubal was worth £250,000, and was drafted in French – a language which Yekini was not literate in – with no lawyer present to advise him on the finer points of the deal. Yekini signed and moved to Vitoria Setubal without receiving his 40 per cent share of the transfer fee. When he eventually confronted club officials about the money, he was told that his financial share of the transfer had been paid to Simplice Zinsou, president of his former club, Africa Sports. Zinsou strenuously denied ever receiving Yekini's share of the transfer fee and suggested he sort out the problem with Vitoria Setubal. Frustrated with the game of musical chairs over who was actually going to pay him the money, Yekini returned to Nigeria informing Setubal that he would never play for them again. There followed a threat from FIFA, at the prompting of Vitoria Setubal, to impose a worldwide playing ban on Yekini, 'For failing to adhere to contractual provisions that he willingly signed.' FIFA chose to ignore the plight of a player and not to investigate the clubs and individuals involved. Yekini had been sold down the river and had to return to Portugal. He currently plays for Swiss side FC Zurich and recently commented in a Nigerian football magazine, 'When I was in Portugal my pay was very poor. Even some reserves were earning more. I thought that this was not fair and that is why I initially stayed away. If I had played for Sporting Lisbon or Benfica, I would not have any regrets.'

In 1993, Dutch football magazine *Voetbal International* stumbled on an African exploitation story. Pint-sized striker Tijani Babangida was signed by Eredivisie side, JC Roda, and eventually loaned out to Second Division Club VVV Venlo. It soon transpired that Babangida was conned by his business manager into signing a carte blanche contract that handed over all of his earnings. Babangida sought the help of the president of the Dutch players' union to help extricate him from his wholly unreasonable contractual situation but when his managers heard this they abducted Babangida and held him hostage in his own house for 24 hours to try and prevent him from incriminating them to the players' union president. Terrified and loathed to involve the police, Babangida settled for the players' union nullifying the contract and he managed to sever his involvement with his 'advisors' – providing them with a let off too.

PSV Eindhoven had been showing a keen interest in Tijani Babangida but changed their minds, on the orders of PSV general manager Kees Ploegsma, as soon as *Voetbal International* printed the story. Jan Leerkess, Amsterdam Bureau Editor, remarked, 'Babangida got himself into a very bad situation. His managers took advantage of his naivity to get the better of him. Our reporter, Wem Raucamp, investigated the story, which made public all the terrible things that were going on.'

Babangida is now in a far better situation and currently plays for Ajax of Amsterdam. He personally confirmed the story in late 1997, tacitly admitting what had been written was true. 'It's something that I really do not like to talk about. I had some problems with my business managers and we had a rather difficult time trying to sort it out. But I am a grown-up guy and I would not find myself in that kind of situation again.'

South Africa, up until the last few years, was in the slow lane of African football. Today, the national team is successful and South Africa has a realistic chance of hosting a World Cup in the not-too-distant future. It's a country that also has its fair share of footballing tales to tell. Until recently, the group of people who ran football were answerable to nobody. These men received vast amounts of money from sponsors and couldn't begin to explain where it was all going. At the start of 1997, Steve Tshwete, South African minister of sport, appointed Benjamin Pickard, one of the toughest judges in South Africa's supreme court, to investigate several allegations of corruption and mismanagement within the South African Football Association.

The judge's enquiry revealed that the previous SAFA president, Solomon Morena, had mysteriously sold virtually every asset owned by the South African Football Association to get his hands on cash. In a deal with Irish-based sports company Awesome Sports International (ASI), the South African FA transferred all ticket rights, advertising sponsorship and television rights to ASI. The annual budget of the SAFA barely exceeded 10 million rand (approximately £1.4 million), so it was peculiar that 28 million rand was suddenly transferred to ASI's overseas accounts. Shortly before the contract with ASI was signed, it was discovered that Brian Mahon, ASI's boss, had given Solomon Morena a 'soft loan' of 500,000 rand to keep him sweet. Foodcorp was another firm anxious that its involvement with the SAFA and ASI should continue so, to make sure, they presented Morena with a brand new Mercedes. Solomon Morena was also found to have raided the SAFA's coffers on two occasions to pay himself what he later called a 'performance bonus' – each payment being 45,000 rand. Funds earmarked for the FA's trust fund were also misappropriated. The final report was extremely damaging. Solomon Morena was earning over 33,000 rand per month and despite resigning over the inquiry's findings he still managed to secure a handsome pay-off. 'I'm not a man of considerable means,' said Morena in response to his departure.

The remaining members of the SAFA's executive committee were left to get on with their jobs, although Judge Pickard warned them that in future no foreign company should be given any South African football rights. The executive committee chose to completely ignore the directive and voted to retain ASI as their marketing company. They had already excelled themselves at the end of the 1996 African Nations Cup in South Africa by awarding each executive Committee member 15,000 rand just for organising the championships – surely a task they were already paid to do.

This is not the only major scandal in South African football. In 1995, Abdul Bhamjee, a one-time publicity officer with the National Soccer League (NSL) was given a jail term for embezzling £1.5 million, money that accrued as TV rights sales for the 1990 World Cup finals in Italy. The scandal began with tales of conspiracy among members of the NSL management committee, and Bhamjee, chairman Roger Sishi and general manager Cyril Kobus were all found to be living flamboyant lifestyles that were well beyond their modest incomes.

All three men were jailed. Bhamjee tried to appeal against his sentence, until it was revealed that he had attempted to suppress the scandal by giving cash bungs to journalists. No serious attempt was made by the authorities to recover the missing money as it is nigh on imposible to recover money that has already been spent. Abdul Bhamjee was recently released from Pretoria Prison, and it would come as no surprise if he managed to make a comeback in South African football.

The usual suspects exist in their droves in the African game, whether playing domestically or abroad. Some are unlucky, some are dishonest and others are naive and to a certain extent victims of circumstance. Etim Esin was an extremely talented football player who could have been one of the greatest players ever to emerge from Africa. However, he had a wild streak that led him to being dubbed 'superbrat' by the Nigerian media, and his actions led to his downfall. Esin's first run-in with authority happened at the end of the 1987 FIFA World Youth Championships qualifiers when he refused to observe squad behaviour rules set out by Nigerian coach Chris Udemezue. Ignoring the players' night-time curfew, he sneaked out of his Lagos hotel room, jumped in his car (which was not supposed to be with him) and drove to a nightclub. Before he reached the club, he was stopped by a group of armed robbers who shot him in the leg and stole his Peugeot 505 saloon.

The media had a field day and Esin's state of health was the subject of nightly reports on the network news. He received unsolicited gifts and mountains of get well cards, while some female admirers even went as far as cooking various delicacies for him. Coach Udemezue was unmoved and unimpressed and told reporters that as far as he was concerned the shooting incident was the final straw and Esin would never be picked for the team again. However, Etin Esin had a lot of friends in high places and they rallied round, ensuring that he went to the 1987 FIFA World Youth Championships in Chile. The tournament was fairly unspectacular from a Nigerian point of view and Esin did not play particularly well. He did attract a lot of attention, though, and an Italian club showed enough interest to tentatively talk terms, only to pull out of the deal when Esin insisted they pay for his girlfriend to travel with him. He eventually ended up playing in Belgium. In November 1991, while playing for First Division side Lierse, he was tested for drug use after a game against Racing Mechelen. Irregularities showed up in the test results but he was discharged and acquitted because of some technicalities in the administration of the test. Esin's luck had held out again – but, alas, not for much longer.

On the field of play, Esin was doing well – so well, in fact, that Portuguese club Braga were anxious to have his services. He travelled to Portugal to talk terms, only to be confronted by journalists with copies of Belgian papers which carried a story that there was a warrant out for his arrest in connection with allegations from a young Belgian girl that she had been lured back to his flat for sex against her will.

So close to a dream move, Braga officials informed Esin that the transfer could not go ahead until he had cleared himself of all charges. They recommended that he return to Belgium immediately. In Esin's opinion, this was far too risky as he almost certainly faced protracted police investigations and, if found guilty, a certain jail term. He later said, 'I could have returned to Belgium to try and clear myself but then they would have put me in a jail first. Even if I eventually got released I would have forever become a jailbird.'

Although he escaped Belgian justice, he didn't escape a worldwide football ban from FIFA. Despite its recent lifting, he has sadly become a shadow of the great player he could have been.

Politics and sport in Africa have a habit of becoming dangerously entwined, and never more so than in November 1995. Nigeria had been heavily criticised by the entire African continent over its deplorable human rights record but the situation worsened on 2 November 1995 when environmental activist Ken Saro-Wiwa and eight associates were executed after being convicted by a Nigerian kangaroo court. The Nigerian military junta were fond of eliminating troublesome elements, despite the fact that Saro-Wiwa and friends were only guilty of protesting against the activities of Royal Dutch Shell.

On the day of the executions, Nigeria played Uzbekistan in the second leg of an Afro-Asian Cup tie and FIFA president Joao Havelange was present as part of his official visit to Nigeria. South Africa were furious, not only because of the executions but because they considered it inappropriate that they be carried out while Mr Havelange was in the country. In return, the South African FA withdrew an invitation to Nigeria to participate in a Four Nations Tournament they were hosting. The furious Nigerians decided to drag the SAFA in front of FIFA's arbitration to claim financial compensation but FIFA ruled in favour of the South Africans, who were let off with a written warning.

That was by no means the end of the incident. The Nigerian government were still seething and, aware that the South Africans were hosting the 1996 African Nations Cup, decided to throw a spanner in the works. As holders of the cup, Nigeria were going to be one of the tournament's top attractions and were much fancied for a third African Nations Cup victory. The Nigerian military junta suddenly claimed that they had received reports from their 'secret agents' within South Africa that an attempt to kidnap or even kill the Nigerian team was likely. The story became public but Nigeria's passionate football fans refused to believe that a withdrawal from the tournament was an option.

To prepare for the competition, the Nigerian team was supposed to set up a training camp in Sittard, Holland, but the European Union had imposed sporting sanctions as a show of displeasure over their human rights record. This meant that the Dutch training camp was no longer an option. The Nigerians tried to go to Israel instead but this too was met with a distinct lack of enthusiasm. Rather like a cornered animal, Nigeria began to talk about boycotting the Championship, putting the Confederation of African Football (CAF) into a state of panic, as it would be the first time in the history of the tournament that the defending champions would be absent and, by definition, unable to defend the cup. ISSA Hayatou, the president of CAF, tried desperately to persuade the Nigerian regime to change their minds. He failed.

General Sani Abacha, leader of Nigeria's military junta, decided the boycott would go ahead and faced a stream of protests from the players. They sought an audience with him at the presidential palace at Aso Rock – in the country's capital Abjua – but were told in no uncertain terms that his decision was final. Cleverly, knowing that the players were bitter about the decision, General Abacha gave them $20,000 each by way of 'compensation'. The Nigerian public were furious with the players for accepting the money, but player Emmanuel Babayaro spoke for the whole squad when he said, 'It is unfortunate that people said that we were silenced with the money that was given to us. We were caught in the middle of a conflict over which we had no control. Left to the players we would have gone to the tournament under any conditions. Watching other nations at the tournament when we should have been there was very painful.'

Punishment from CAF was swift in coming. Nigeria were banned from the 1998 and 2000 African Nations Cup and fined $15,000, although following an appeal the player ban was reduced to just the 1998 African Nations Cup on compassionate grounds. After boycotting the 1996 African Nations Cup, the Nigerian government imposed a total media blackout on the tournament, depriving all Nigerian football fans from watching the event on television.

Nigeria also came very close to being banned from the 1998 World Cup finals as there were calls for the CAF ban to be extended worldwide. Only an appeal organised by Ajax star Sunday Oliseh, on behalf of the players to FIFA, stopped this from happening. In a passionate plea, the players said that their careers could be ruined, through no fault of theirs, if they were denied a chance to show their skills in France. According to Oliseh, 'The consequences of being out of the World Cup were too terrible to contemplate, so I and my team-mates got together and wrote to Joao Havelange. We were quite fortunate that they were kind enough to listen to our plea. The careers of several Nigerian players could have been destroyed if they had banned us.'

This was not the only run-in FIFA had with the Nigerians. The 1995 FIFA World Youth Tournament was due to be held in Nigeria and it would be the first time the tournament had ventured to a sub-Saharan African country. Naturally, the Nigerian population was looking forward to having a global soccer festival on their own doorstop, so it was extremely disappointing when it became apparent that the tournament stadia were in a generally poor state of repair. Ample time had been given to prepare facilities but Jack Warner, president of the Central American and Caribbean Soccer Federation (CONCACAF), commented that it would take the 'eighth wonder of the world' for Nigeria to be ready for the tournament.

At the same time, letters had been sent to FIFA by pro-democracy activists in Nigeria, warning that if the participating teams went ahead and played in the tournament, their lives could not be guaranteed in the unpredictable political atmosphere that prevailed in Nigeria. FIFA grew nervous and started to search for a reason to take the tournament elsewhere. Salvation came in February 1995 when an outbreak of cholera – close to one of the tournament venues – allowed FIFA to withdraw Nigeria's hosting rights on health grounds. The resident representative of the World Health Organisation in Nigeria claimed that the outbreak was not as serious as was first claimed but FIFA stuck to its guns and issued another statement on 27 March 1995 stating that 'security considerations' compelled them to move the tournament to the Gulf state of Qatar. In a blow to the Nigerian government, it was obvious that the pro-democracy activists' letters had done the trick. In an attempt to get their own back, some of the activists were arrested for 'an act of sabotage', which sees them languishing in Nigerian jails to this day. Justice Nigerian style.

Accepting a job in African football can be rewarding but it can also be dangerous and sometimes even life threatening. As we have seen, Clemens Westerhof was successful on the pitch but somewhat careless off it, and he is certainly not alone. Unorthodox is a word that sums up French coach Phillipe Troussier and his time in Africa. Troussier is one of the oldest coaches in Africa and has managed Asec Mimosas of the Ivory Coast, Kaiser Chiefs in South Africa, Fus Rabat in Morocco and Credit Agricole FC, also in Morocco. He also managed three national teams during his African experience, piloting Nigeria to the 1998 World Cup finals. Of his own admission, Troussier learnt a lot, and now considers himself more open and able to understand and tolerate people who have a completely different attitude to himself.

Having led Asec Mimosas to a League and Cup Double in the Ivory Coast, he was invited to take over as coach of the Ivory Coast national team, The Elephants. His main task was to ensure qualification for the 1994 World Cup finals in the United States but the fact that they were drawn against the might of Nigeria in the qualification rounds made it almost impossible. Troussier, renowned for his forthrightness, said publicly that his team did not have the capacity to defeat Nigeria and therefore he was unsure about the Ivory Coast's chances of qualifying for the 1994 World Cup. His candour was too much for the Ivory Coast Football Federation to take and without hesitation they sacked him.

After another spell in club football, Troussier took over as Nigerian national coach in March 1997. He only lasted six months and described the experience as his most trying period as a manager in Africa. When he negotiated the deal with the Nigerian FA, it was agreed that he would receive an upfront payment of $30,000 to cover his salary for three months. After that, he would be paid $10,000 per month. The Nigerians failed to honour their promise of monthly payments and when Troussier left the job in October 1997 he was still owed the outstanding money. He reported the Nigerian FA to FIFA for breach of contract but the matter has still not been settled.

Money was not the only problem. Troussier complained that the endless bickering among officials made his job very difficult. 'Only a cowboy can manage in Nigeria,' says Troussier. 'Could you imagine that they wanted me to submit my team list to the "technical committee" which had to vet my selections before I could use the team that I wanted to! I couldn't tolerate that because I think that would compromise my integrity as a coach, so I had no choice other than to leave.'

Troussier's detractors labelled him a tough but very stubborn man, and he admits that on occasion he had to resort to unorthodox methods. 'Some people say that I am a stubborn man, a difficult man. But if they call me that for the simple reason that I am demanding for my rights or that of my players, then so be it. If I have to climb to the top of the tree and cry out for my rights, I will be willing to do that if, at the end of the day, I achieve what I want.'

German-born coach Reinhard Fabisch is one of the most eccentric characters working in African football. He used to be the manager of the Zimbabwe national team, The Warriors, when they had a slim chance of playing in the 1994 World Cup finals. Zimbabwe were playing Cameroon in Yaounde and needed a draw, which they failed to get. Fabisch was furious with the officiating Gambian referee, A. Faye, who he claimed had been bribed to give important decisions in favour of Cameroon. So he ran on to the field, showering the referee with a wad of Cameroon franc bank notes, a rather direct way of making his point. FIFA took a very dim view of such an unsubstantiated allegation and banned Reinhard Fabisch from international football for a year.

Dave Roberts is one of the few British coaches to have worked for long periods in Africa. His professional career started in 1960 as a player with Liverpool before moving on to Tranmere Rovers, Wigan Athletic, Altrincham and then Morecambe as player/manager in 1972. His coaching career has taken him to Kuwait, Zambia, Saudi Arabia and several clubs in South Africa. In South Africa, Roberts remembers the National Professional Soccer League suffering from a plan to form a breakaway league. The breakaway faction involved Abdul Bhamjee (also involved in the TV rights scandal), who at the time knew he was about to be banished from South African League football. He tried in desperation to set up the National Soccer League to continue his involvement in football. Roberts was manager of Bloemfontein Celtic and his chairman was not very keen to join the rebels but he was also afraid that his club may lose out as some of the other big South African clubs were anxious to join.

Dave Roberts was sent to represent the club and the chairman's interests at a committee meeting. To the assembled club representatives, Abdul Bhamjee announced that Cyril Kobus would be involved (Kobus was also involved in the TV rights scandal) and planned to hire all the office staff from the National Professional Soccer League to help administrate the breakaway league. Many of those office staff were suspected of illegal activities and the delegates knew it. It was suggested that a new set of office workers be employed but Bhamjee said this was impossible as he had already promised them the jobs available.

The league was set up and the opening game was to be between the Orlando Pirates and Jomo Cosmos. It was no ordinary game. The Orlando Pirates presented two teams for the match as rival factions in the club had different ideas as to who should play. Three players from the Pirates team that had the backing of the fans ran across to confront one of the players from the old Pirates team. This player was then stabbed by one of the three players. The man staggered away and managed to clamber over a barbed wire fence. If he had been caught, he would not have escaped alive.

The breakaway National Soccer League had started typically and badly. Roberts thought it was odd that Abdul Bhamjee, a man who had just served a jail sentence for corruption and embezzling, should be the public relations officer for the new league. 'He was probably the only public relations officer that I have ever known that signs cheques for the league and has a key role in all its financial transactions,' says Roberts.

When Dave Roberts was manager of Bloemfontein Celtic, he took his two small sons to a game against African Wanderers. When he arrived at the ground he was asked bluntly whether he could help African Wanderers 'achieve the right result' because they were in danger of being relegated. Roberts said he could not, informing the Wanderers representatives that the only way they were going to win was to play better than his team.

Roberts sat with his sons and the chairman during the game, which went well from his point of view; Bloemfontein Celtic were winning 1-0. Sitting on the far side of the ground, Roberts remembers seeing a large crowd gathering behind them as the game was drawing to a close. Roberts asked his chairman what was going on and was informed that they were in danger of being lynched because they had not let African Wanderers win the game. The chairman suggested that they start walking towards the main stand so that they could make a quick getaway if need be. When the whistle blew, a gang of African Wanderers fans ran towards them and Roberts, the chairman and the two boys had to dive into a police wagon for safety. Eventually, the police regained control of the situation and managed to rescue Roberts' players, who were stuck under the main stands besieged by an angry mob.

Corruption in African football is not just the sole domain of South Africa and Nigeria. Algeria got in on the act in April 1997. Three club chairmen went public on alleged corruption within the country's football league. It started when Kacem Eliman, chairman of MC Oran, accused Abdelmajid Yahi, his opposite number at US Chaouia, of having asked him to lose a match between the two sides in exchange for arranging for a third club, Usm Ein Belda, to allow Oran to close the gap on their points deficit. Eliman also accused the referee of pocketing $1,600 from US Chaouia to make sure that Oran did not win. Furious about the allegations, Yahi said that it was Kacem Eliman, in front of four witnesses, who had tried to bribe him with a payment of £20,000 to let Oran win the game. He was also offered ownership of four swanky apartments as a sweetener, he claimed.

The situation grew increasingly confusing, with claim followed by counter claim being bandied about. Then 'Soussou' Boulabib, the chairman of the then League leaders, CS Constantine, threw his hat into the accusation ring by claiming that Kacem Eliman tried to fix the result of another key League match for £40,000. Former top administrators and current international referees were also accused of taking bribes. The Algerian Football Federation did their best to get to the bottom of the allegations but nothing has been proved. However, there's no smoke without fire and recent stories in the Algerian media suggest that the National League Championship has been 'fixed' for the last six years.

Uncompetitive football has also attracted corruption, a good example being the Zambian national team's efforts to play friendly matches against the Ivory Coast and Ghana in November 1997. Zambia were due to play Ivory Coast on 2

November and Ghana on 5 November, but the Ivorian and Ghanaian Football Associations claimed that they had never entered into any correspondence with the Football Association of Zambia and consequently refused to make their national teams available for the so-called friendly tour.

Luckily for the Zambians, Burkhard Ziese, their manager, had coached the Ghanaian national team in the past and used his connections within the region to organise three friendly matches. They were beaten 1-0 by SOA of the Ivory Coast and 3-0 by Ghanaian Hearts of Oak. The Zambians only defeated another Ghanaian side, Great Olympics, by virtue of an own goal. The botched trip raised a lot of questions in the Zambian media. President Frederick Chiluba, Zambia's leader, gave sports minister Samuel Miyana seven days to explain what had happened to the US $50,000 of Zambian taxpayers' money that had been earmarked for the tour.

The minister failed to explain what had happened to the money but Matthew Mulwanda, general secretary of the Nation Sports Council of Zambia, heaped the blame on the Zambian Football Association secretary, James Mazumba, who apparently did not seek the council's approval for the trip and only submitted the forms after the team had departed the country. Zambian FA boss Teddy Mulonga made a public apology for the scandal but failed to unearth where the money actually went. Once again, an African football financial scandal had been swept under the carpet.

Ethiopia is not a country that trips off the football follower's tongue but it has a fairly buoyant domestic scene and its national team regularly takes part in the African Nations Cup. Given the ongoing social problems in Ethiopia, it is understandable that when the national side plays abroad players can become tempted by foreign lifestyles. Seeking a better life in Europe, sixteen members of the Ethiopian national squad absconded from their team hotel in Italy, where they were in transit for an African Nations Cup qualifying game in January 1998. Some of the players never returned home but others came to the conclusion that Europe was not the Eldorado they thought it was. Ethiopian Football Federation technical director Getahun Gebre-Giogis and his two assistants, Neguise Gebre and Tesfaye Gebru, were sacked over the incident.

The rivalry in Egyptian football is as fervent as in any other country but has a worrying level of fanaticism among some fans. Suspected corruption among officials has given rise to a situation where no Egyptian referees are sufficiently trusted to referee impartially. European referees are employed to take charge of many games, especially the big ones. Cairo clubs Al Ahly and Zamalek have a fierce rivalry and they met in the 1996/97 season in a match that was a Championship decider. Mohammed Higazy, a 45-year-old Al Ahly fan, was killed together with his entire family when they were attacked by their Zamalek-supporting neighbours. This was all before a ball was kicked.

When it comes to player discipline, the Egyptians take some beating even if it means cutting off their nose to spite their face. Hossam Hassan, an incredibly talented player, is regarded as the *enfant terrible* of the Egyptian game and was banned from playing for the national team because he assaulted a team official. The incident took place shortly before the 1990 African Nations Cup finals and although he was one of the Egyptian team's key players, the Egyptian FA refused to lift his ban.

African football, although sometimes dishonest, promises

much and one day will deliver. To go forward it must rid itself of cowboy administrators, corruption and an inferiority complex that verges at times on paranoia but the continent is football crazy, and its talent exists in abundance. Its finest hour may not be too far away.

3 Superstition and the Occult

SKILL, BRAINS AND STAMINA are what it takes to win a game of football. But human beings, being what they are, always look for that little 'something extra' to make the difference between success and failure. Without doubt, footballers are among the most superstitious living things on the planet. Fans, too, are certain that that Panatella in the pub before kickoff or those lucky pants can mean the difference between victory and defeat.

So, is there anything significant in these rituals or is it just a load of mumbo-jumbo? Some very big names diligently stick with their pre-match rituals, some through habit but most through fear of failure. Gary Lineker never used to shoot at goal during the pre-match warm up and always got a haircut if he was off form. Teddy Sheringham puts his right boot on first without fail, while Chelsea's Mark Hughes does exactly the opposite. Central defender Neil Ruddock insists on following the player wearing the No. 10 shirt out on to the pitch, an action no doubt made more difficult with the introduction of the Premier League's bizarre squad-numbering system. And what on earth would he do if Liverpool's No. 10 broke his leg and was out of action for six months?

Ruddock's Anfield team-mate Rob Jones always touches the famous 'This is Anfield' tunnel sign before trotting out to do his stuff. The innocent shinpad is another football accessory that can apparently have an effect on a game's result – Barry Venison always put his right boot and shinpad on first – as is the shirt. Paul Ince puts his shirt on in the tunnel. Newcastle's Warren Barton only puts his shirt on *exactly* five minutes before a game. United's Andy Cole always comes out last from the tunnel. Insisting on the same position in the team line when they run out on to the pitch isn't unusual. Former Crazy Gang member Alan Cork was always third and Kerry Dixon was fourth in line with ball in hand. Former player turned pundit Tony Gale wore his watch for the warm-up, religiously left the field exactly fifteen minutes before kickoff, and removed his watch precisely ten minutes before a ball was kicked in anger. Ronnie Whelan, who played with distinction for Liverpool and the Republic of Ireland and then went into management with Southend United, only shaved on a match day.

It's not just at the ground that players exercise their superstitious ways. Some, like Norwich City's Ian Crook, insist on wearing the same suit for the next match after every victory. Ex-Scotland goalkeeper Alan Rough could quite easily claim to be the most superstitious player ever in British football. His build-up to any game he was playing in was truly bizarre. Rough insisted on having a shave every match-day morning, and he always carried an old tennis ball and a key ring with a thistle motif to the ground. He permanently had a miniature football in his pocket, found on the grass in his goalmouth one afternoon. He wore a star-shaped medal, always used peg 13 in the dressing room and wore his original No. 11 shirt from his first club underneath his jersey. As if that didn't guarantee enough luck, he always bounced the ball off the tunnel wall three times before he went on to the pitch and kicked the ball into the empty net as he ran towards the goalmouth. He also had a habit of blowing his nose as often as possible during a game, keeping a special supply of handkerchiefs under his cap for this purpose. Good goalkeeper though he was, Rough was never consistently outstanding and will probably be remembered as one of a long line of fairly average Scottish goalkeepers. Or was he just plain unlucky?

The curse of *Hello!* is well documented, but for footballers there is an even greater fear. Five Premier League stars, worth £50 million between them, have all been sidelined with serious injury since the BBC featured them in *Match of the Day*'s opening sequence for the 1997/98 season. The unlucky five, namely Alan Shearer, Roy Keane, Robbie Fowler, David Seaman and Ian Wright, surely can't put their accidents down to coincidence. That's not fear of drying up you can see in the eyes of any player or manager who appears on the show – it's fear of the *Match of the Day* curse.

Gordon Taylor, chief executive of the Professional Footballers' Association, sympathises. 'Players are very superstitious, doing things like putting a certain boot on last or putting their shirt on last when they get changed for a game. Superstition is rife in football because it is a game that needs quite a bit of good fortune as well as skill.

'It would not surprise me to see those players who appear on *Match of the Day*, and are still fit, asking to be removed. It might sound light-hearted but nothing is light-hearted in football where luck is a serious business.'

A *Match of the Day* spokeswoman said at the time, 'When

we decided to do the opening we picked out the most prominent people. It's just the nature of football that players get injured. To say that it's a curse is a little harsh.'

People often say that football is a religion and some may be sincere in their claims. Religion has a part to play in football although it's true interpretation is as diverse as it is certain. The Pope, the Head of the Catholic Church, used to be a goalkeeper in his youth – apparently he was good on crosses. Dr George Carey, the Archbishop of Canterbury, is football mad and he follows Newcastle United with a passion. Clubs have their own chaplains and some use religious belief to frighten the life out of their players. Italian Serie 'C' side Viterbese scared the living daylights out of their players to try and end a losing streak. They planted eleven crosses in the centre circle, each with a player's shirt number on it. They won their next match.

Barcelona Football Club celebrated 39 years of playing at the famous Nou Camp Stadium by holding a mass in the club car park. Throughout Catalonia, paintings of the last supper were replaced by posters of Ronaldo (now with Inter Milan) to bring good fortune to the Catalan club.

Apparitions even play their part in the beautiful game. The Virgin Mary was seen hovering three or four metres above the pitch during a match in Gradina in northern Croatia. Local priest Father Biber, who claimed similar events went unreported during the 1950s, said, 'Some of the children who saw her say she was bowing her head. Others claimed that tears were coming from her eyes and her hands were clasping rosary beads.'

In Britain, the finest example of religion, superstition and possibly darker forces coming together involves Birmingham City Football Club. A band of travellers used to live on the land that since 1906 has been known as St Andrew's, the home of Birmingham City. The club forcibly threw the travellers off the land and, it is said, incurred the wrath of the malevolent spirit of a dead gypsy. The gypsy swore that nothing but bad luck would befall the club and history suggests that there could be something in it. Birmingham City, save for one or two exceptions, are a club starved of success.

Everything possible has been done to try and rid the curse once and for all. St Andrew's has been exorcised countless times and ex-manager Ron Saunders even ordered the soles of the players' boots to be painted orange in a bid to ward off any evil spirits. More recently, ebullient manager Barry Fry decided that he and his players should urinate on all four corners of the pitch in a truly bizarre anti-occult ritual. It may have worked, as Fry took City to Wembley for the Auto Windscreen Shield final while he was boss.

While many football fans occasionally believe that their club is cursed, Birmingham City supporters have to live with the certainty, week in, week out. An enterprising Blues fan once grabbed a lump of concrete while renovations were being carried out at St Andrew's and threw it in the concrete mixer at Aston Villa where the Holte End was being rebuilt. The theory was that Birmingham's bad luck would switch to Aston Villa. Well, it *was* only a theory.

At the beginning of the 1996/97 season, Karen Brady, Birmingham's chief executive, designed the club's kit and added an ecclesiastical element in the form of a dog collaresque white band around the neckline. But not even divine intervention can help them it seems. They still haven't won a major trophy or managed to reach the Premier League, and until they do the gypsy's curse remains.

Further afield, countless Latin players affirm themselves with the sign of the cross when entering the fray or even celebrating goals. In Turkey, sheep's blood is seen as a good luck charm, and sheep are sacrificed regularly with the blood daubed on the players' faces. British players Dean Saunders, Les Ferdinand and Barry Venison, who have all played in Turkey, found the whole ritual bizarre to say the least. 'Thank goodness that sort of thing never happened at QPR,' remarked Ferdinand.

In South America, occult rituals can take on worrying connotations. In 1996, the president, fans and directors of Colombian club Deportes Pereira organised a ceremony to ward off evil spirits after a dead black chicken was found in the directors' box. The animal was found strung up with lighting cable at the club's Heran Ramirex Stadium. Three bags containing earth from a nearby cemetery were also found arranged in a line, together with some odd markings. Whatever the gruesome collection meant, the club were rightfully wary, especially as they went on to lose thirteen out of their first fourteen League games.

Nowhere in the football world is more steeped in the occult than Africa. The diverse cultures give rise to different forms of magic and curses, and the belief in the power of what the West would call 'witch doctors' is very strong. Doubters mock at their peril, say the locals.

Trailing by a lone goal against Ghana during a 1980 African Nations Cup group game in the Nigerian city of Abadan, a bunch of irate Guinean players interrupted play for several minutes, insisting that the referee order goalkeeper Carr to remove his cap, which they were convinced had been enhanced magically to prevent him letting in goals. The Guinean players were incensed that the referee took no notice of their protest, undoubtedly blaming their eventual loss on the power of headwear.

Christopher Ohenhen, the Nigerian striker who plays for Spanish side Compostela, refused to play for his national side until fairly recently because he was convinced that one of his international team-mates, who he refused to identify, had the power to cast a spell on him which would make him play badly and ruin his career in Europe.

It could be coincidence or it could be evidence of supernatural forces at work in African football but the story of Tanzanian international goalkeeper Pondamali is interesting. Pondamali had a suspected 'magic talisman' confiscated by the referee in an African Champions' Cup match against IICC Shooting Stars in the 1970s. A talisman is an object made by a juju man (witch doctor) to fulfil whatever wish the owner desires. Juju men are revered in many parts of Africa and their powers are said to be extraordinary. There had been a number of reports and rumours that Pondamali had a talisman and often buried it just behind the goal line. In the match concerned, he was indeed spotted hiding something between his goal posts at the Liberty Stadium in Ibandan. The eagle-eyed player informed the referee, who stopped the game to make a thorough search of the goal area. A juju talisman was found and confiscated while Pondamali, who was famous for his tremendous athleticism, seemed to become a completely different player straight away. His form took a big dip and he was never quite the same player again.

Of course, not everyone believes in such 'dark' powers. Dutch coach Clemens Westerhof, who manned Nigeria's national team and several club sides, found a pot of juju prepared by a mystery Juju man dumped in front of his

Lagos home as he was leaving one morning for work. He asked one of his domestic staff to remove the pot but no-one was willing to even touch it. Westerhof decided to move it himself but was informed by his driver that if he touched the pot he would die. He remembers the incident: 'I told them that it was just superstitious nonsense. I kicked the thing to the other side of the street and that was the end of it.'

In the Ivory Coast, there is a famous juju man called 'the Gbass of Daby, well known for his preparation of magic potions which are used by players keen to win matches at all costs. His antics are the stuff football legends are made of and business is booming. The Gbass prepared a magic juju pot for the Ivory Coast national team just before the 1992 African Nations Cup in Senegal. The potion was paid for with taxpayers' money at the direction of Rene Diby, the Ivorian sports minister. The Ivory Coast played their first match against Ghana and won a ludicrously high-scoring game, the final score being 10-9. They did not win the Championship, though. Perhaps the juju wasn't strong enough.

Four years later, the 1996 African Nations Cup finals were held in South Africa. The Gbass of Daby was asked by the Ivorian government to concoct another of his juju potions, but his prices had gone up so it was decided they could do just as well without. The Ivory Coast performed woefully and were dumped out of their tournament in the first round.

French coach Phillipe Troussier, who is well versed in African football, says the locals were convinced of the power of juju. 'I had a lot of problems with Rene Diby, the sports minister, who believed that without juju, there was no way that my team could perform. I tried to let my players know that they needed to develop a professional attitude to succeed in football,' he said. 'As far as I am concerned, people are entitled to believe in whatever they want. In my opinion, all talk of juju is just a matter of psychological warfare. If people believe that if they slaughter a dog before a game it will guarantee victory, I guess that they are entitled to their belief.'

Gary Bailey, the former Manchester United goalkeeper, admits to using juju in the seasons he played for South African side Kaiser Chiefs. Although sceptical about its effectiveness, Bailey felt that in African football using juju was essential. Maybe there was something in it – the Kaiser Chiefs won every domestic trophy while Bailey was playing for them.

Invariably, if a team loses form African fans do not call for the head of the manager or the resignation of the board but lay the blame firmly at the door of the team witch doctor. Yet fans are reluctant to publicly criticise the offending guru for fear of attracting bad luck.

It is claimed that there are many ways a witch doctor can influence the outcome of a match. High on the agenda for a witch doctor is putting a spell on his own team to inspire them to a superhuman performance. Or he can bewitch the opponents, slowing them down and interfering with their co-ordination. Referees have been singled out for special attention too.

The *pièce de résistance* of the witch doctor is to apply his powers to the match ball, as happened in the case of Wilfred Phiri. He was a goalkeeper who conceded twelve goals in one game and claimed that his calamitous performance was down to the fact that he saw several footballs at once and did not know which one to save. Phiri was adamant that his opponents should not take the credit for putting the ball past him a dozen times – in his opinion, the other team had used witchcraft. Even if it is psychological, it clearly works.

The 1988/89 season in Zimbabwe was a campaign littered with unplayed fixtures because some clubs would rather forfeit a match than face the superior juju of their opponents. One team took a 50 mile detour on their way to a Cup tie to try and negate the effects of any witchcraft being placed on them. Not surprisingly, they lost the game largely due to the extended journey endured in sweltering heat.

Another team ran out on to the pitch spinning in tight circles, waving their arms in the air and chanting mystical slogans. This was designed to give them immunity from their adversaries' magic. Once again, it didn't help. They lost.

It's certainly true that witchcraft does not guarantee success. One club in Botswana made a large advance payment to a witch doctor in return for his help in a forthcoming match. The club lost the match and sued the witch doctor to recover the money. The case reached Botswana's high court, where it transpired that the witch doctor had concentrated his efforts on making the goalkeeper impregnable by sitting him in a tin bath filled with cold water and throwing tennis balls at him. This was to ensure that he would play brilliantly even in the most adverse conditions. Farcically, the goalkeeper contracted influenza and spent the match shivering, sneezing and conceding five goals. The team won the case and recovered their money.

In the early 1990s, the African Football Association started to wake up to juju and its influence on the continent's game and began to frown on its use. In 1990, four players from Tongara, a First Division team in Zimbabwe, were banned from football for life by the Zimbabwe Football

Association. The players had followed their witch doctor's instructions and urinated in the opposition goalmouth prior to the second-half kickoff. Nelson Chirwa of the ZFA urged players to think carefully before using suspect witchcraft in future. He said, 'I would advise all teams to go to a better witch doctor rather than indulge in such disgusting acts.'

His advice was followed by Mhangura, an unfancied team who, before a game against Zimbabwe champions Dynamos, used a slightly less revolting way of bewitching their opponents. They drove a herd of donkeys across the pitch. It paid off – they drew 1-1. But Shepherd Murape, the Mhangura manager, regretted that due to lack of transport they would not be able to take the animals to away matches.

At the Houphouet Boigny Stadium in Abidjan, Ivory Coast, on 2 May 1993, the hosts were playing a World Cup qualifier against Nigeria. A pot-bellied Ivorian witch doctor, naked but for a loincloth, sauntered on to the pitch balancing a large earthenware pot on his head filled with his magic potion. After performing a frenzied dance which he claimed woud invoke the spirits of defeat on the Nigerians, he then proceeded to urinate on the pitch to ward off the spirits of defeat for the Ivory Coast.

Unsurprisingly, the witch doctor's antics left the Nigerian team feeling slightly edgy, so much so that they refused to shake hands with the Ivorian prime minister, Allasane Quattara, preferring to bow instead during the pre-match pleasantries. Stephen Keshi, the Nigerian captain, had given his players strict instructions not to have physical contact as he was convinced that Quattara's hands had been dipped in a juju man's magic potion, which would only be effective if he touched the opposition. The Nigerians' preventative measures did them no good: they lost the game 2-1.

The return match was to be played at Nigeria's national stadium in Lagos on 23 September 1993, and few gave the Ivory Coast any chance of victory because Nigeria had not lost at home for eleven years. The Ivorians enlisted the help of juju man Gbass of Daby, who was instructed to prepare a bag of charms which would ensure defeat for Nigeria. However, the only way to make the magic work was to smuggle the potion on to the pitch so that the required ceremonies could be performed. The Nigerians had heard on the grapevine that the Ivory Coast team had enlisted the Gbass to work his magic and issued directives to Nigerian customs officers to thoroughly search the Ivorian contingent on their arrival at Lagos Airport. Despite furious protests, the team were detained for over two hours and searched, and the magic potion was located and confiscated. No magic, no win – Nigeria won at a canter by four goals to one.

Nigeria and the Ivory Coast clashed again on 6 April 1994 at the El Menzah Stadium, Tunis, in the semi-finals of the 1994 African Nations Cup. Some of the Nigerian players went for a wander on to the pitch before the game and discovered that several raw eggs had been broken and placed on the turf – a ritual that is supposed to bring bad luck.

In desperate need of an antidote, the Nigerians went to a local Catholic church for some holy water to sprinkle on the pitch. As one Nigerian supporter at the stadium put it, 'This is a battle between the forces of good and evil. And since we are on the side of good, God will give us the victory.'

God must have been listening. The Nigerians came back twice after being behind to level the scores, finally eliminating the Ivory Coast in a tense penalty shoot-out.

Zambia were Nigeria's opponents in the final but were no match for them as The Eagles notched up their first African Nations Cup title in fourteen years.

Not all officials and fans embrace magic and witchcraft, however, and often good old-fashioned faith can almost make sense where normal reasoning cannot. Raifu Oladipo, chairman of the Nigerian Football Supporters' Club, firmly believes in the power of prayer and the fact that God *does* take sides in football matches. He claims that while he was asleep he got a message from God that Nigeria were going to lose their 1994 World Cup tie against Italy. 'During the night before the game, I received a vision that we were going to lose the match. In the dream, I recall being in a room where we were celebrating our victory, only for someone to tell us that this was not the place that we were meant to be,' says Oladipo.

'When we went to the area that was prepared for us (in the dream), I discovered that we were all mourning and I wondered why our mood had changed so suddenly. When I sat down to interpret the dream, it was my understanding that we would come close to victory but we would be beaten at a very crucial moment.'

Oladipo assembled all the members of his supporters' club in Boston to tell them what God had revealed to him but their confidence was unshaken. 'When we managed to hold on to a 1-0 lead with only a few minutes left, I thought that I had misinterpreted the dream I had, but as soon as the Italians made the incursion that enabled Roberto Baggio to score a goal, I told my members that this was going to be the equaliser, so it was no surprise when it happened,' remembers Oladipo.

Nigeria's match with Brazil in the semi-final of the 1996 Olympic football tournament was another occasion when Oladipo and his chums sought divine intervention. A special session of fasting and prayers was planned to ensure that

Nigeria won the match. Oladipo recalls, 'Brazil had been a thorn in our flesh for a long time. I cannot remember the number of times that they have ruined my appetite for food. When we were trailing 3-1, I recall some of the Brazilian fans going round the stadium inviting people to join them when they have a big party to celebrate their Olympic football title, as they believed that defeating Argentina in the final was a foregone conclusion. Some of my members were downcast but I told them to keep on praying and singing their praises to God, as I was confident that the Lord would give us that day. I had a vision of victory in my dreams the day before and God never disappoints me.' Nigeria won and went on to beat Argentina in the final. Oladipo and company must have been praying hard.

British coach Dave Roberts, who has worked all over the developing football world, spent the mid to late 1970s coaching in Kuwait before moving to Zambia and South Africa in the 1980s. He returned to the Middle East in the mid 1990s. In football terms, Roberts had seen it all, and he has witnessed first hand the peculiar goings on in the uneasy marriage between witchcraft and African football. In the Middle East, religion comes before football every time.

Kuwait is a predominantly Muslim country and Roberts remembers well his first encounter with local culture and its relationship with football. 'We were preparing for a game in Salmiya. All of us went into the dressing room and after a few minutes I suddenly realised everyone had gone. It was empty. I was a bit surprised so I said to this chap, "Where has everybody gone?" and he said, "Captain's outside," and I said, "Outside for what?" He opened the dressing-room door and showed me outside. I saw about 3,000 people on their knees praying. I asked him, "Where is the team?" and he pointed and said that they were in the crowd. He then pointed out the other team who were praying with another 3,000 people. When I asked him, "What are they all doing?" he informed me that they were all praying for victory in the game and that it would be good for all of us. I jokingly replied that since both teams were praying for victory, we might as well go home since the match was going to be a draw!'

Roberts was aware of the strict religious observance in a country like Kuwait but was still shocked to see his team praying with the crowd rather than getting into the right frame of mind in the dressing room. But he says, 'If prayer is the key to victories, then maybe we should all start praying!'

He speaks glowingly of the Kuwaiti fans, who are very different to the Europeans. They are extremely vociferous and if their team gets a good result they go wild, jumping up and down on the tops of expensive cars and blaring their horns at all hours of the day and night. 'They are a very warm people,' says Roberts.

But it is not all plain sailing. Coaches in Saudi Arabia are faced with different problems than those they have been used to. During Ramadan, the Islamic fasting season, games begin at midnight, with the players allowed something to eat shortly before kickoff so they are strong enough to play. The matches end at two or three in the morning. To the Saudis it is a perfectly normal way of life and something that foreign coaches have to adapt to.

Dave Roberts has also been the victim of players seeking his removal from a club by fairly unorthodox methods. 'There was one player at my last club (Abdu Setar) who was heard asking Allah to engineer my dismissal from the club,' says Roberts. 'When I confronted the player, he didn't deny it. My first reaction was that I didn't want anything to do with this guy. The president of the club, who was a really shrewd administrator, backed me up so we disciplined the player for his attitude. He eventually came to his senses and pleaded for forgiveness. We gave him a second chance and he turned out to be one of my best players.' Allah must have been proud.

On the football side of things, Africa is totally different. Roberts has managed five African clubs in various parts of the continent and became aware of the muti (juju/witchcraft) very early on in his managerial career. Many Africans claim not to believe in the power of the muti or juju, but Roberts thinks they only say that because they really believe that it does work. Double bluff, then?

For a year Roberts managed the South African team Orlando Pirates, in Johannesburg. Muti was extremely important to them and they would go to considerable lengths to invoke its power. When the squad were staying in a hotel prior to a game against the Kaiser Chiefs, the players made a small fire in one of the hotel rooms. 'They threw something into the fire, which was obviously producing "the muti" for them,' says Roberts. 'They all stood around the fire with their heads under some blankets so they could inhale the smoke and fumes from the fire.'

Unbeknown to the players, the room contained a smoke alarm which decided to make its presence felt. 'After the alarm went off everybody was ordered to clear the hotel. The players were still doing the rituals when the hotel manager caught them in the act. He was so angry that he threw them out, so we had to book into another hotel that night,' remembers Roberts.

The same players were involved in a similar incident in

their dressing room before a match. Dave Roberts remembers smelling smoke and feeling one of his legs getting hotter and hotter. Not realising at first that the players had started a muti fire, Roberts enquired whether the dressing room was on fire. One of the players told him to look behind him, where the muti fire was beginning to burn brightly.

Roberts' attitude to such rituals was liberal to say the least. 'As a coach, I don't care what the players do. My job was to get results and if the people believe that the muti will help them get the results, then I am all for it. I'd even pay for the muti if it will achieve the right results. It really doesn't bother me. It used to be quite expensive to buy the muti potion. We had it sent in from Swaziland which was apparently *the* big muti area. If you had muti from Swaziland, they reckoned they were on to a winner because it was considered to be the best type of muti available for South African players. Some people used to travel up to Swaziland to get the muti two days before the game. It was a real event and it was certainly not something to be taken lightly. They really believe in it and who am I to complain? If it achieves the results, then I am all for it.'

Roberts categorically denies that he ever paid a muti man for his services, although he does admit to being involved in some of the ceremonies with the players. While he did not mind a limited involvement, he drew the line at parting with his blood, however. There were occasions when players inflicted cuts upon themselves, then bathed in various juices and concoctions, presumably to try and acquire the muti power very quickly. Roberts stuck to Radox in his bath.

Some teams believe in the power of muti more than others. While still managing the Orlando Pirates, Dave Roberts remembers a particularly big game against the Mamelodi

Sundowns, who used to be managed by Clemens Westerhof. At the time they were coached by Stanley 'Screamer' Tshabala, the former South African national coach.

'Screamer believed in muti so much,' says Roberts. 'Although my team were believers, it wasn't as much as his, probably because I was the coach. We were playing this game at the FNB Stadium in Johannesburg. The whistle was blown on six or seven occasions to signal the players to leave their dressing rooms, but the players did not come out. This was a very big match that got major television coverage but neither team was willing to follow the route to the pitch that the other team would be using. Both teams feared that their route would be strewn with a secret muti potion that would have a detrimental effect on their performance.'

Both sides ended up making completely different entrances on to the field of play.

Kaiser Motaung, the owner of the Kaiser Chiefs, was acknowledged as a highly intelligent man, and his belief in the power of muti was nothing short of incredible. At the Kaisers' training camp in Johannesburg, Motaung's favourite muti man was a regular visitor. Yet for all the power that Motaung believed muti had, he was also terrified of it being used against him. He had an argument with the chairman of Bloemfontein Celtic, who warned Motaung that if he did not back off over the dispute he would dispatch someone to Lesotho to prepare some muti that would 'take care' of him. The feud was quickly settled, such was Kaiser Motaung's fear of muti and its power.

It is well known that his team were frequent practitioners of muti, and even the white players used to join in. Neil Tovey, a former captain of South Africa, was certain the magic did not work but joined in because, in his words, 'If it is good enough for the other members of the team, then it's good enough for me.'

Dave Roberts managed the Zambian club Konkola Blades between 1980 and 1984 and witnessed the use of magic and rituals on numerous occasions. His team regularly refused to change in their dressing room because they were scared that their opponents had put some damaging muti in the room. Snakeskins and dead rats were put over his team's dressing-room doors and powder was spread along the pathway the players used. The powder may have been harmless but Roberts' players took its meaning and threat very seriously.

Occasionally, magic can go embarrassingly wrong. In the Ivory Coast, the man who was supposed to administer a charm got very upset that he did not get a game in the 1989 Ivorian Cup semi-final between African Sports and his own team, Stella. The player, who came from the juju man's home town, was the only one who could sit on the bench and perform the incantations. Stella surged into a 2-1 lead and held it for most of the game and the said player was told that he would not be needed on the field. In a rage, he smashed the witch doctor's charm into small pieces. Within seconds, Africa Sports had equalised. To add insult to injury, they cracked in the winner right on the final whistle.

It's not just the players who rely on the power of magic. Supporters also swear by muti and juju as a way of influencing a football match. However, let us not forget that there are those who refuse to acknowledge it at all.

One such character is 68-year-old Gani Elekuru (aka Baba Eleran), whose fanatical passion for the Shooting Stars club has turned him into Nigeria's best-known football supporter. An ordinary man who started out as a butcher in the meat markets of Ibadan in western Nigeria, he has followed Shooting Stars for well over two decades. Chairmen and coaches come and go but Baba Eleran is seen as the everlasting symbol and is regarded as an integral part of the club. He claims to have no interest or belief in juju and its power but firmly believes he has an alternative gift – as an amateur prophet.

Some of his exploits are well known among the locals. It is said that before a League match against Shooting Stars' arch rivals, Rangers International of Enugu, Baba instructed Taiwo Ogunjobi, a club official, to tell the captain that if he won the toss he should choose the west end of the pitch for the first half. He stressed that if Shooting Stars did start from the west end, the first half would be goalless but they would score twice in the second half. Shooting Stars won the toss and obediently chose to start from the west end. They won 2-0 with two second-half goals. If only it always worked like that.

Journalist Tunde Omo Adelakun knows Baba Eleran quite well and on one occasion stayed at his house, only to be woken in the middle of the night by what he described as 'Arabic-sounding incantations'. He asked Eleran what he was doing. Eleran was trying to find out what the players should and should not do so that his results predictions would come true.

Adelakun says that Baba Eleran is slightly cagey about whether the players take his advice. He told him: 'Some of them do. One day, I told a striker to lash out at an opposing defender if he was fouled in the first ten minutes, and that if he didn't do so, this defender would harm him. The player felt that I was giving him bad advice and he ignored me. He was carried off in the thirteenth minute with a gashed head.' Spooky.

It would be a foolish football fan who dismissed the power of muti, juju, black magic or even God – after all, you never know when you might need one or all of them. And even if they don't work, they can certainly influence the mental state of some of the protagonists. It is also entirely understandable that countries incorporate strands of their culture into football.

Thiam Belafonte is the editor of the Ivorian club ASEC Mimosa's fanzine and he feels that it is as simple as people needing to believe in something. Belafonte says, 'I can recall an incident where an official, who knew that his players believed in juju, played a trick on them. He put some perfume in a bottle of water, making the players believe it was some kind of magical potion. He shook it vigorously and then gave it to the players to apply on themselves. They believed that it would help them and they went on to win the match 5-0!'

Mind power 1 Juju 0

4 Asia

THE 2002 WORLD CUP FINALS will be shared between Japan and South Korea. However, the 1998 Asian stock market collapse could affect the build-up to the finals although FIFA have received repeated assurances from the hosts. Money, and lots of it, controls world football, and the costs of staging a major Championship are staggering. It is easy to see how richer countries can afford to be reliable hosts while poorer countries will look at the prospect rather like a frightened rabbit in a car's headlights. A further dose of economic ills in south-east Asia could put the 2002 World Cup in jeopardy and force FIFA to relocate to another part of the globe. The FA recently denied that England has been put on standby, but there's no smoke without fire.

An Asian World Cup would undoubtedly boost the region's love affair with football – which is already considerable. Hong Kong, Vietnam, China, Japan, Malaysia and Indonesia all have national leagues which provide nurseries for the future Asian football explosion. Players nearing the end of their careers have been enticed to Japan to play in the 'J' League – earning big money and cashing in on their fame off the pitch with numerous business and promotional ventures. Absorbing the culture has never been top of their agenda, despite what they may say.

European football is very popular in Asia, particularly the English game. Interest in the FA Premier League is massive, not only to the Far East fans but to the gambling syndicates that wager fortunes on the outcome of matches. TV coverage of live games has encouraged this boom industry. It's a murky world full of unpleasant characters who list deception, intimidation and even murder among their specialities. In early 1998, Malaysian police claimed to have smashed an illegal, multi-million pound football betting business operating via the Internet (an indication of how sophisticated the syndicates have become). The police arrested two men and seized computers, printers, faxes and phones in a raid on the gang's base.

If the tentacles of the syndicates have spread to Britain, as many suspect, it is much harder to prove. In August 1997, Bruce Grobbelaar, Hans Segers, John Fashanu and Malaysian businessman Heng Suad Lim were acquitted by Winchester Crown Court on charges of match fixing. The prosecution were convinced that the three footballers had conspired to fix matches because of their contacts with Asian betting syndicates through intermediary Heng Suad Lim. The original charges against the four men were made in November 1994 and sent more than a ripple of fear through the English game. Video evidence of certain matches and goals scored or conceded made up a large part of the prosecution's case together with a video tape showing Grobbelaar and his former associate, Chris Vincent, discussing certain events that took place in matches. During the trials, Grobbelaar and Segers admitted taking large sums of money for forecasting results – a clear breach of FA rules

– but denied fixing any match for their own financial gain. Fashanu remained silent throughout both trials. Heng Suad Lim was totally acquitted although Segers, Fashanu and Grobbelaar were charged by the FA over their breaching of FA rules. 'They have admitted the breaches of relevant FA rules at the trials,' said David Davies, the FA's director of public affairs. 'It was announced that Sir John Smith would advise the FA on what action to take in relation to the evidence presented at the trial. Bruce Grobbelaar and Hans Segers have been charged with breaches of FA rules on betting.'

Alarm bells rang over this case, despite the fact that they were found not guilty. The potential for corruption seemed great and suspicions rose over the involvement of the Asian syndicates in England.

It was not until the former Czech midfielder Michel Vana was arrested that the saga began to unravel. Vana was charged in August 1994 with attempting to fix six matches in Malaysia's sixteen-team professional soccer league. For quite a few years Singapore was integrated into the Malaysian semi-professional league. It was only as gambling and corruption became more and more of a problem that the Singaporeans took the decision to sever their football ties with Malaysia. The split was acrimonious and led to the formation of the 'S' League in Singapore. This is the league that still exists today although the standard of football is very poor. The British equivalent would be the Isle of Wight setting up a separate Premier League to compete with the existing one.

At the time of his arrest, Vana was playing for Singapore and his activities brought shame on the well-ordered society that prevails in the tiny republic. The police claimed that he had pocketed over £60,000 from his activities and were confident that a trial would result in his conviction. However, the authorities made the mistake of giving Vana bail, which he used as an opportunity to flee Singapore. The trial never actually took place and a few weeks later he popped up in the stands of his favourite Czech club in Prague, seemingly oblivious to the charges against him in Singapore. Vana still evades arrest successfully but his activities in south-east Asia set the police on the trail of a web of bribery and corruption which continues to haunt Asian football.

Across the causeway in neighbouring Malaysia, detectives launched a nationwide investigation into Vana's activities and football corruption in general. It quickly became the biggest and most thorough inquiry in the history of the professional game. But as leads were followed up, the detectives soon realised that, due to the complications and secrecy behind the corruption, they were out of their depth. Bribery was so insidious in the semi-professional Malaysian game, virtually every player in every team in the Malaysian League was involved. Incredibly, the police delayed their swoops on suspects until the 1994 Malaysian Cup tournament was over because they genuinely feared that there would not have been enough players left to compete had they acted earlier. Initially, players and officials from the losing semi-finalists were targeted and the police estimated that up to 90 per cent of League and Cup games were fixed. In some cases, the entire first team of suspected clubs were rounded up for police questioning. Most of those players were eventually released although 80 were subsequently banned from football. Twenty-two individuals were exiled under emergency laws dating from the days when Malaysia was a British colony. The laws allowed the police to send offenders to remote districts of Malaysia – mostly jungle areas – under a specific law called the Restricted Residents Act. The authorities, although moderately successful in weeding out Malaysian football criminals, knew they had not totally eradicated the problem. In the mid 1990s it was widely believed that four bookmaking syndicates were still trading in Malaysia, the curse of corruption refusing to lie down.

It is a great irony that in a region so obsessed by gambling, betting on the outcome of football matches is illegal both in Malaysia and Singapore. The only gambling concession is to non-Muslims who are allowed to bet on horse racing but nothing else. However, actually enforcing the law is a whole different ball game. In fact, it's virtually impossible. The enthusiasm of the Chinese, who form the bulk of Singapore's population, makes the police's job even more demanding. Illegal bookmaking has become almost a cottage industry in Singapore and it is easy to see why. It wouldn't be much of an exaggeration to say that the Chinese are willing to gamble on which of two flies will be first to leave a wall. Millions of pounds in bets are wagered every Saturday afternoon on football. Colonial links mean that for decades bets were placed on the outcome of English League matches and it was only when Malaysia's semi-professional league started that punters began to switch their betting allegiances. Local form was easier to understand and gamblers became very adept at taking the bookmakers' money. Predicting results became second nature and the bookies panicked and turned to corruption to try and stem their losses. They bribed players in order to achieve profitable match results. Clandestine syndicates who singled out key players and paid them handsomely for their help and co-operation were formed.

Initially, their tactics were fairly straightforward. Goal-keepers were paid to dive the wrong way and strikers encouraged to shoot wide of an open goal. A lot of the players were relatively poorly paid and jumped at the chance to increase their income. Frequently, one syndicate would pay a certain team in a match to lose while another rival syndicate would be paying players on the same side to try and win. Players recruited from overseas could not believe what was going on. One, who wishes to remain anonymous, summed up the situation: 'Never before in my career had I taken to the field with my team-mates knowing the match result in advance.' Foreign players were attractive prey for the syndicates, as Australian Alan Davidson, an apprentice with Nottingham Forest who later joined the Malaysian team Pahang, remembers all too well. Davidson was approached personally by one of the illegal bookmakers and asked to throw a game. 'He offered me 20,000 Singapore dollars (at the time about £10,000) just to make one mistake, to enable the opposition to score. He said it didn't matter how I made the mistake, just as long as they scored one goal – $20,000 was mine on the table.'

Davidson refused the offer, much to the runner's displeasure.

Getting to the bottom of the marriage between match fixing and gambling in south-east Asia was virtually impossible. A number of coaches grew suspicious of their teams' erratic performances but found it very hard to pinpoint the cheats and their cheating. On the face of it, a mistake is a mistake and to differentiate between an honest one and a deliberate one is hard. Douglas Moore, former coach of the Singapore national team, said, 'I used to sit on the bench and see something happen and think, Is that straight? Was something going on there? Because the honest mistake gets wrapped up with the deliberate mistake and you just don't know which is which.'

A third party observer could be forgiven for interpreting the situation as relatively harmless but, given the vast sums of money at stake, the syndicates were very well organised and often linked to sinister underworld gangs. One such syndicate was masterminded and controlled by a 50-year-old blind man who had never seen a football match in his life and he made an estimated £5 million a month from football matches in Malaysia alone. With business strewn around other parts of south-east Asia, his yearly take was reputed to be in the region of £2.5 billion a year. He operated out of a relative's business premises in Kuala Lumpur and was obsessive about keeping his identity a secret. Other king-pins running rival syndicates were equally publicity shy and were only known by nicknames such as The Banker, The Uncle, The Godfather and The Short Man.

Loose talk can jeopardise whole syndicates and their corrupt money-making operations, so trust is essential, particularly when there are hundreds of bookmakers involved. The Short Man is the head of the most powerful syndicate of them all and he and his cronies are widely believed to have rigged a six-team tournament in Malaysia a few years ago. The tournament featured some extremely dubious results and incidents which raised suspicions among Malaysian football experts. But it was the same old story: everyone knew what was going on but nobody could prove it.

Very little is known about The Banker other than the fact that he is extremely rich, corrupt and secretive. Intelligence sources firmly believe that he is a resident of Indonesia and during the Hans Segers/John Fashanu/Bruce Grobbelaar and

Heng Suad Lim trial, Lim admitted in court that he had received large sums of money from an Indonesian man called Johannes Josef. It is possible that Josef is the infamous 'Banker'. Josef was never called to give evidence at the trial and kept a low profile around the time of the match-fixing revelations in England. These syndicates are so rich that it would not be uncommon for high-ranking syndicate members to buy season tickets and executive boxes at British Football grounds. These individuals think nothing of jetting to Britain for a day to watch a game and then fly out to their next destination. Occasionally local nationals are used to represent the Indonesians but more often than not the Godfathers make their own appearances. The plan is to slowly infiltrate major English clubs by playing up their wealthy images. If money goes to money it will not be long before the syndicate will be welcomed into a big club or clubs, albeit unwittingly.

Buying the services of team members can often be all too easy but occasionally the runners can come up against less willing parties. Player Douglas Moore recalls such an incident. 'I have seen $50,000 in a suitcase. I can't say where, but it happened in Asia. It was offered to my former boss, before I joined Singapore. The money was to lose the game by a certain scoreline. We were going to lose anyway, but they wanted us to lose by, if my memory serves me right, four-nil. My boss said no. At half time they increased the offer to $50,000 a goal ... making a total of $200,000. Again we said no.'

Such fortitude in the face of such temptation is admirable although probably rare. Asian journalists have reported locally that many coaches have been guilty of taking cash bungs. It is entirely possible that corrupt coaches have bribed their own players to achieve a result desired by a syndicate's runners.

The links that the Far East syndicates have with organised crime are considerable and ultimately helpful. Drug pushing, money laundering and prostitution are a useful way of supplementing their already huge incomes. Also, having the support of organised crime groups means that a prison sentence does not spell the end of their operations. Mafia gangster Al Capone conducted his criminal activities from his prison cell for many years and it's the same for the syndicate members. Malaysian police openly admit that it makes very little difference if gang members are in or out of jail.

Anyone who decided to double cross one of the syndicates or even try to expose them to the police plays a very dangerous game indeed and there is no question whatsoever that the syndicates would kill to protect their interests and empires. One anonymous footballer was left under no illusions that a gang meant business when he opened his car door and found a cobra coiled on the passenger seat. Lazarus Rock, a Malaysian sports journalist, knew that he was getting a little too close to the truth when he received a letter containing a stick of chalk shaped like a bullet. The accompanying piece of paper contained a chilling threat: 'The next one will be for real.' Rock was also approached some months later to pass on a warning from one of the syndicates to a British journalist who was making a nuisance of himself with his enquiries.

In a bid to eradicate corruption, Malaysia decided to scrap their semi-professional league and set up a totally professional league instead. Not surprisingly, it failed to remedy the situation. Johnson Fernandez, who writes for the *Malay Mail*, sums up the current situation. 'I thought the situation would have improved when the game turned professional in Malaysia. But for every dollar you pay the players the syndicates will offer them ten. They have total control of the game.'

An easy illustration of the seriousness of the situation comes from former player Alan Davidson, who recalls a game against Brunei which was postponed halfway through because of monsoon rains. 'We went to have a meal at a local hotel and some people came up and said, "Well done. You won four-nil." We said, "No. We have to replay tomorrow night." The next day we won four-nil.'

Football corruption in south-east Asia has now become so absurd that for many it is difficult to take it seriously. One newspaper featured a cartoon of a man being carried shoulder high by a group of triumphant footballers, cheering, 'We won!' 'Who's that?' inquires the referee. 'Their coach?' 'No,' says the linesman. 'It's their bookie.'

Singapore has played host to a number of football corruption trials. A recent one heard claims of clandestine meetings in underground car parks, brown envelopes stuffed with cash and coded offers being made to players on their pagers. The trial ended with one of the syndicate's high-ranking big timers, 36-year-old Rajendran Kurusamy, otherwise known as 'Pal', being sentenced to six months' jail in Singapore. Kurusamy is a small, moustachioed man with a penchant for hugely expensive gold rings and very mean bodyguards. He became an illegal bookmaker in 1994 and is rumoured to have made at least £10 million within the space of a few months taking bets on the English Premier League and local games. When asked how he made so much money in such a short period of time, Kurusamy was brutally frank. 'I fix football matches to ensure that I win my bets,' he said. A full investigation into Kurusamy's activities was carried out by Singapore's *The New Paper*, who disclosed his methods for fixing local games. Kurusamy would approach different teams in the League and tell the players how he wanted them to play, instructing them very specifically. If we wanted one team to score more goals than the other, he would tell them to 'go all out' safe in the knowledge that the other side would co-operate because he had bribed them as well. Having two teams in his pocket allowed Kurusamy to be virtually certain of success.

Kurusamy's passport shows that he was in certain cities at the same time as key World Cup matches. Other important international sporting events have also been watched in person by Kurusamy, leading to speculation that his interests lie not solely in football. He is almost certainly the man who approached former referee Ken Aston, one of the most respected people in world soccer before his retirement. Aston was on holiday in Singapore with his wife, son and daughter-in-law when he was targeted by Kurusamy. He was approached by two men of Indian extraction in a restaurant and offered £25,000 in cash to pass on the names, addresses and telephone numbers of top Premier League players and senior referees. The men told Aston that they were prepared to gamble up to £450,000 on the outcome of English Premier League games, and if successful expected a return of about £3 million. They stressed to Aston that they needed a cast-iron guaranteed correct score to bet on and indicated that they were extremely keen to recruit him as their middle man to fix matches with players and officials. Apparently, their own attempts to break into English football had been thwarted by the high salaries of players in the Premier League but they had far from given up and would be in

London in the not too distant future to establish further contacts. Ken Aston returned to his hotel room to fax FA chief executive Graham Kelly under the heading 'Attempted bribery'.

A shocked Kelly informed the police who in turn tipped off their colleagues at Interpol. However, it is understood that Interpol's enquiries reached a swift dead end – such is the syndicate's ability to cover their tracks.

British police were alerted to a new scenario in the Far East gambling syndicates' pursuit of corruption in December 1997. A series of floodlight failures during Premier League games shown live on television aroused suspicions that something untoward could be going on. On 13 August 1997, the floodlights failed at Derby County's Pride Park Stadium during a game against Wimbledon. The match was eventually abandoned at 9.32 p.m., even though the power had been restored, because referee Uriah Rennie decided that it was too late to continue. An investigation found that the floodlight failure was caused by an incorrect setting on a circuit breaker in the main sub-station. It was the first game at Derby's new £23 million stadium.

On 3 November 1997, the London derby between West Ham and Crystal Palace was abandoned because of floodlight failure with the score at 2-2. The live televised match was plunged into darkness after 65 minutes and the club's electricians failed to solve the problem. Seven weeks later, on 22 December 1997, the lights failed when Wimbledon played Arsenal at Selhurst Park, a match also live on TV. Darkness fell on the ground one minute into the second half with the score at 0-0. Wimbledon owner Sam Hammam called for an urgent Premiership investigation into floodlighting throughout the country. Hammam said, 'The first failure at Derby was bad. It was even worse at West Ham and now it is a disaster. It is very embarrassing and something positive must come out of this evening.'

With so much money swilling around in English football, it is inconceivable to many that multiple stadium floodlight failures manage to occur. To others, the explanation is simple: the floodlight problems can be directly attributed to the Far East gambling syndicates. On Christmas Eve 1997, the *Express* claimed that the syndicates were behind the spate of floodlight failures in the Premier League. The claim was that a bookmaking network stretching from London to Gibraltar to Singapore knew hours before kickoff that Arsenal would not be allowed to win the match against Wimbledon at Selhurst Park. The Premier League announced on 23 December 1997 that they were launching an inquiry into the technical reasons behind the embarrassing floodlight failures and the police also launched an investigation into the possible link between the failures and the Far East gambling syndicates. Superintendent John Lansley ordered the investigation and began by trying to ensure that any evidence that the lights were tampered with was not destroyed by electricians repairing them. 'We need to seize the part that broke down. If we don't move quickly that could make an investigation very difficult,' he said.

Police were never called to investigate the two other failures at Derby and West Ham because the clubs were satisfied they had found the cause of the faults and there didn't seem to be any suspicious circumstances behind them. Of course, it would be naive not to take into consideration the fact that the syndicates could easily hire an undercover electrician to do their dirty work and cover his tracks sufficiently well. Doubts about the validity of the Selhurst

Park floodlight failure were raised when a highly respected former British betting industry worker, who insisted on anonymity for fear of reprisal, told the *Express* that he was going to the game but was advised to forget it because it was a fixed match. 'I was told there was no way Arsenal would be allowed to win on the night,' said the source. 'I was told it might be another "West Ham". It was nothing to do with gambling in this country; it was big Far East stuff.'

The man, who had been employed by a London spread betting firm, confirmed that British bookmakers were not involved in the scam. He claimed that he had received a warning about the Wimbledon–Arsenal match from a source in Gibraltar. 'There is a network amongst us blokes who work in the industry and we talk. I heard from Gibraltar that Monday's match was fixed.

'In Singapore, Hong Kong and throughout Malaysia they are mad about English football and even madder about betting. Normally, a match like Wimbledon–Arsenal is worth about £60,000 to a London spread betting firm, while in the Far East it is worth millions. Out there they bet on a straight win, lose or draw and, of course, most of the money was on Arsenal as the favourites. The bookies don't want them to win and make sure they don't.'

In the Far East, a result stands providing at least half the match has been played, which could explain why, when the score was 0-0, the lights failed a few seconds into the second-half. 'If Arsenal had been winning the lights would have gone out before half time,' suggested the source. 'If Wimbledon had been winning they would have stayed on. As it was level at the start of the second half, whoever the bookies have got did his stuff.'

At the West Ham–Crystal Palace match, the Far East

bookies would not have wanted a West Ham win as they were favourites. As soon as West Ham equalised to make the score 2-2, the lights went out. In the Far East, the half-time score of 2-1 to Palace would be the final result and the bookies would clean up.

The bookmaking syndicates target one-off midweek matches because the money staked on a single game is very high compared with a Saturday when there are many games. The police inquiry barely got started and, apart from establishing whether there was any tampering with or sabotage to the equipment, it was doomed to fail. How can a British inquiry possibly hope to explore syndicates and their godfathers from thousands of miles away when the local Asian forces only enjoy very limited success? There was never any suggestion that the clubs or their ground staff were involved but experts felt that it would be relatively easy for outsiders to tamper with electrical circuits. The company that installed the Crystal Palace lighting system expressed surprise at its failure and agreed that deliberate sabotage should be considered as a cause. Interestingly, despite Selhurst Park's slightly run-down appearance, the ground's lighting system was acknowledged as being one of the best in the country and had experienced no problems since its installation in 1990.

The experts questioned the other matches too. Ian Major, sports lights business development manager for Philips Lighting, Britain's leading supplier, said, 'It is extremely unusual for three Premier League games to be abandoned so close together – all the more so with two of them on TV.

'The only good news for us is there was nothing wrong with the equipment we installed, which means they had some sort of mains power failure. It's surprising for this to happen so suddenly, when they've had nothing wrong at Selhurst Park in the seven years since the system was put in.

'West Ham's problem was equally surprising,' said Major. 'They had been going for around four and a half years without a problem. There are any number of reasons for floodlighting to be knocked out, but the most obvious one is for their power to be halted when one of the many fuse systems is blown. Wanton vandalism could be to blame but that would obviously be extremely dangerous.

'What is unusual is all three have been in the same season in the same league. These are relatively new systems; they shouldn't be breaking down.'

The situation seems clear cut. Either the syndicates managed to arrange the failure of the floodlights through paid saboteurs in England or it is the most amazing coincidence. The former bookie who spoke to the *Express* has no doubts about what is really happening. He has indicated that he would be prepared to give evidence on what he knows to either the Premier League or the police. 'It all stinks.' he says. 'I like a gamble like the rest but I also love my sport and this sickens me. I didn't believe it at first, but it makes sense.'

No further floodlight failures have occurred since the last one in December 1997 as no doubt much more attention was paid by clubs to their lighting systems following the furore. By the same token, the syndicates could have made three enormous wins and changed tactics.

The FA Premier League ordered a separate investigation into the facilities and provisions relating to electricity supplies to all Premiership grounds. A team of specialist consultants were asked to examine the state of electrical equipment, the provision and use of back-up generators and the demands on the supply, particularly during televised games. Any club that fails to fulfil a fixture for whatever reason is in breach of the Premier League rule book. Officials are told to take further action if any Premier League club's facilities are found wanting.

Attempts are being made to try and curb the power and influence of the gambling syndicates. Singapore and some other countries in the region have now decided to lift their ban on betting and plans are underway to introduce a UK-style football pools in an attempt to undermine the illegal bookies. Asian football supporters like Douglas Moore believe that such a move could quite possibly save football in south-east Asia. 'The bookies have so much money in their hands that they're able to fix the result of a game. But once you legalise betting then I think that you will kill all that. People can have a bet and the odds will be just as good legally. And the people they bet with legally are not going to go around trying to fix the outcome of matches.'

The bookies' influence is so pervasive that it is difficult to imagine them disappearing. Many observers fear that the syndicates will start to look elsewhere – and that the English game could be at the top of their agenda. Journalist Johnson Fernandez explains why the syndicates have turned their attention to England: 'The local soccer public is well educated when it comes to the Premier League and they can read the form – which isn't good for the syndicates, which have been losing a lot of money. That is why I think the syndicates have switched their attention to the English game.'

People like Fernandez are convinced that the bookies' influence on English football is pretty insignificant at present but it is thought that attempts have been made to infiltrate the lower divisions so as to gain a foothold for the ultimate prize – the Premier League. Fernandez insists the process has started but at the moment only involves a handful of matches. 'But,' he warns, 'don't forget that is how it started here.'

We have been warned.

5 Gambling

I N BRITAIN, betting on the outcome of football matches is a £1 billion a year industry. China and many south-east Asian countries are also big gamblers not just on football but just about anything that has a pulse and moves. Fans and players alike enjoy a bet, but players are not allowed to bet on football matches. Of course, it's an unenforceable rule because players could ask a relative or friend to place a bet for them – and some do.

Following the Bruce Grobbelaar, Hans Segers and John Fashanu court cases where all three were charged, together with Asian businessman Hen Suan Lim, of match fixing, the Football Association has appointed Sir John Smith, a former deputy commissioner of the Metropolitan Police, to conduct an inquiry into betting and forecasting in football. Segers and Grobbelaar were also the subject of a further FA inquiry, despite their 'not guilty' verdicts in the law courts, as the sports ruling body alleged that they had been betting on matches. The FA felt that football was in the dock and needed to be exonerated. Sir John Smith's goal would be to clear football's name and convince supporters that football in Britain is fair and honest.

Those same fears exist all over Europe – with some

justification. Dynamo Kiev were briefly banned from European football for trying to bribe a referee with furs and former Swiss referee and French minister Bernard Tapie was jailed for match fixing and financial mismanagement at Olympique Marseille. A number of Cyprus internationals have been accused of betting that their team would lose a World Cup game against Bulgaria in 1996.

FIFA, the governing body of the world game, are notoriously bad at admitting to problems in football but even they have felt compelled to set up a panel to study how to fight corruption. Somewhat surprisingly, it was the mandarins at Lancaster Gate through Sir John Smith who were able to reveal their findings first. Smith's two-month inquiry discovered 'widespread betting which is damaging to the integrity of professional football'. During his investigation, Sir John learnt of cases of people betting on their clubs to lose games. He said that betting 'has the potential for, and can be seen as, creating a serious distraction from the underlying principles of any sport – namely "playing to win".'

The existing FA betting rules are straightforward enough – FA members are not allowed to bet on matches except through the Pools, although there is no rule against forecasting. However, several players have cheerfully admitted to betting with bookmakers on which of them will score the first goal in a match. Wimbledon's 1988 FA Cup-winning side did it, as did John Scales during his time at Liverpool. They are by no means alone.

Sir John Smith's recommendations were threefold. The FA should, he said, distinguish between, 'Secret forecasting of results for the purpose of betting and the public forecasting of results.' Secondly, he advised the FA that all professional players should be given a copy of the FA rules and for clubs to be responsible for ensuring that they are understood and complied with. Finally, he wanted the betting industry to report direct to the FA on any gambling activity carried out by those involved in the game.

In return, the FA promised to deal with transgressions more seriously than in the past. Sir John stressed that he had received no information that betting was used as a vehicle for 'corrupt practice'. He said, 'It may be the case that all betting, albeit forbidden by the rules, is otherwise innocent with its participants having no thought of corruption or match fixing. However, I am not persuaded that particular bets, such as first player to score, could not provide temptation to some people.'

In November 1997, Tottenham midfielder David Howells claimed that players use 'spread betting' to gamble on football and that he had witnessed actions from opposing teams to influence the results of bets. 'Bets were placed on the first dead ball,' he said. 'Teams would come to us, and if they won the toss, kicked to touch.' What a cosy way to make money. Although a relatively new form of gambling, spread betting is increasingly popular. Gamblers predict the number of corners in a match, the number of yellow cards or even the time of the first throw-in. Spread betting companies offer punters a 'spread' which they can either bet above or below. For example, the spread for the total number of yellow cards in a game might be 3.5–4.5. Punters who think there will be lots of yellow cards will bet above the spread, while those who think the card count will be low will bet below.

David Howells talked specifically about players betting on the time of the first throw-in (the spread might be 30 secs to one minute) and whacking the ball directly into touch from the kickoff to claim a hefty profit from the bookies.

The success of spread betting has been marked. City Index was the first company to offer the service and spreads were applied to numerous sports. In an interview with TV's Julian Wilson, City Index's Paul Austin was asked what the most popular betting subjects were. 'Football first, football second and football third,' was his reply. Sporting Index was first to devise markets on such novelties as the number of corners in a match and the combined total of the goalscorers' shirt numbers. Early casualties included one punter who lost £500,000 by persistently overestimating the number of corners in top matches.

If it happens at a football match, you can spread bet on it. Nottingham TV engineer Paul O'Carroll bet on the time of the first throw-in before the Euro 96 match between Portugal and Denmark. When the ball went out of play, he was convinced that he had won 227 times his original stake. However, Sporting Index said they had reviewed the time of the throw-in because the referee made the player retake it when a fan threw a sandwich on the pitch. Mr O'Carroll was £400 worse off. Precision is the key to spread betting. In the match concerned, the time of the first throw-in is calculated by when it is taken, *not* when the ball goes out of play.

Spread betting firms remain vigilant for irregular betting patterns. Such a situation occurred in November 1996 before an FA Cup second round replay between Wycombe Wanderers and Barnet. Hill Index announced that it would be reviewing its policy of offering bets on the time of the first throw-in after it issued a spread on the time of the first throw at 60–75 seconds. They were deluged with calls from clients eager to bet on the first throw-in happening before 40 seconds had passed on the clock – a spread 'down' of 40–55 seconds. The betting paper the *Racing Post* later claimed that when the ball was played down to the Wycombe left wing seconds after kickoff, sections of the crowd chanted, 'Out, out, out.'

Hill Index admitted to the *Racing Post* that the betting patterns on the time of the first throw-in were very irregular. The amounts were unusual too – the vast majority of bets were usually between £1 and £10 but this time they were much larger sums. No large-scale sums of money were paid out as the ball did not go out of play until 51 seconds and was thrown back into play eight seconds later. At the other extreme, the first ball to go out of play can take an eternity. In the Euro 96 match between Scotland and Holland, nearly ten minutes had passed before the first throw-in.

One game in the 1996/97 season between Manchester United and West Ham attracted attention when West Ham's Paul Kitson kicked the ball into touch after just seven seconds. Prior to the match, spread betting firms took evasive action after receiving several phone calls. The punters were told that they wouldn't be offering a price for such a bet as they feared the throw-in market was open to manipulation. West Ham manager Harry Redknapp told the *Racing Post* at the time, 'It's a very dodgy bet and I suppose it could be open to manipulation.'

Spread betting, accumulators, win doubles and trebles, score forecasting – punters can bet on almost anything and by any method they wish. The bookmakers have made it easier and easier for fans to part with their cash. The industry is more and more sophisticated in its methods and football's unpredictability provides the incentive to gamble. However, football gambling has not always been so popular or hi tech. The earliest instance of betting occurred before the Football League was even established. Bets were placed on the first FA Cup Final between Wanderers and the Royal Engineers. The Royal Engineers were made the 4/7 favourites but went on to lose the match 1-0. Betting on football matches quickly became very popular and in 1887 the *Birmingham Post* reported that working men had bet a whole week's wages on the outcome of the West Brom v. Aston Villa FA Cup Final. What today is known as fixed-odds combination betting only developed with the establishment of the Football League in 1888.

By December 1889, the forerunner to the football pools was being touted by a Blackburn bookmaker – the universal football and prize coupon – which had a wholesale and a retail distribution. The idea was simple. Agents were signed up to spread distribution and increase the pot of prize money available to the gamblers. Around the same time in Manchester, an enterprising early bookmaker offered punters £25 if they could predict the correct half-time and full-time score in the FA Cup Final between Blackburn and Sheffield Wednesday. The bookmaker got lucky. Blackburn won 6-1.

The Football League got wise to the ethics of the situation in 1892 by banning all players and officials from betting on matches. In 1902, the Football Association extended the ban to everyone who attended a football ground. The House of Lords also stuck their oar in, appointing a Select Committee to report on betting, particularly illegal cash betting. The 1893 Betting Act prevented all bookmakers from keeping a house, office, room or other place for betting purposes and they were restricted further in 1906. The Street Betting Act prohibited bookmakers from operating on the street, so to carry out their business they had to be both subtle and resourceful. But gamblers were very determined. Betting in the army and in pubs was rife, and many landlords ran football-based lotteries in their hostelries. A survey in Liverpool claimed that 250,000 fixed-odds betting coupons were collected in a single week. Demand was big but the process of betting was clandestine and difficult.

A couple of British companies based in the south of England devised an ingenious way to operate. Layfield Brothers and White Fisher began to run their businesses from the Continent, distributing betting coupons throughout England in envelopes printed with a return address in Flushing, Holland. However, Dutch authorities came under intense pressure from the British government and were eventually persuaded to stop aiding British bookmakers in 1911, who simply upped sticks and moved to Geneva to carry on their business. After the First World War, the Ready Money Football Betting Bill was introduced, forcing punters to pay for their coupon bets a week in advance. In 1920, Jervis of Birmingham became the first significant football pools operator, launching a coupon where customers could attempt to forecast the outcome of groups of matches for a guaranteed cash prize. Littlewoods of Liverpool launched their pools service in 1923, operated by three wireless telegraphists including John Moores. They distributed around 4,000 coupons outside grounds in the Manchester area in February 1923, only to have the wind taken from their sales when 35 were returned. They tried again with another 10,000 coupons – this time a disastrous 'one' was returned. John Moores was determined to make a success of the venture, eventually buying out his two partners. It was a gamble that worked, as by 1926 turnover was a healthy

£2,000 a year. More pools companies were launched as Vernons, Zetters and Empire Pools all started trading between 1929 and 1935. The week in arrears payment method was altered in 1954 under the terms of the Pools Betting Act which was passed by Parliament. This act made it legal for stakes to be sent in to pools companies with current coupons. At the beginning of the 1960s, licensed betting offices were legalised with William Hills paying over £1 million to fixed-odds coupon winners in September 1961. By 1962 it was estimated that up to twelve million Britons were playing the football pools each week. The Pools Panel was set up in 1963 and featured ex-players Tom Finney, Ted Drake, Tommy Lawton and George Young, who all cast their expert eyes over postponed games to determine results. Maudling effectively killed off the mass popularity of fixed-odds betting in 1964 when he slapped a 25 per cent tax levy on gamblers. In one form or another, the pools survived although the pools companies had to tempt the public to part with their hard-earned cash. In 1969 Littlewoods launched 'Trap the ball', the first spot-the-ball competition. It took until 1986 for the first million pound pools winner to emerge – nursing sister Margaret Francis, together with ten colleagues from Roundway Psychiatric Hospital, Devizes, Wiltshire, won £1,017,890 when their eight from eleven perm hit the jackpot. The winning numbers were selected by the group's patients!

In Scotland, gambling rules are very specific for players, who face a lifetime ban for betting on a match in which they are involved. England is more tolerant, with players often backing a colleague to score the first goal. The Football Association banned bookmakers from offering odds on individual matches following the Sheffield Wednesday match-fixing scandal in the 1960s. The newly introduced rules allowed wagers on match results only on three or more games. Single bets on Cup games were still allowed as the general feeling was that there was more at stake in a Cup match than any money won from the bookies. It was not until 1991 that the FA allowed single bets on matches, but they had to be shown live on TV. They also permitted first and last goalscorer, correct score, half-time and full-time scores, again only for TV games.

Gambling is easier and easier to do in the nineties. Its attraction is obvious and to some it can become an uncontrollable illness. Its compulsiveness has led to many players' downfalls. Horse racing is very popular among the footballing fraternity and big names are heavily involved with the sport. Mick Channon, Kevin Keegan, Niall Quinn, Mick Quinn and David Platt are just a few names who own or train race horses. The appreciation of the sport of kings can be put down to anything from a general affection for the sport through to a useful way to fill a few hours in the afternoon after training. Some players are open about their gambling while others employ private bookies, the latter being a useful way of gambling if the player is overseas. Private bookmakers have been used in recent years by at least three foreign-based British internationals who regularly faxed their wagers from abroad. One international was rumoured to frequently bet tens of thousands of pounds on horse racing and lost telephone number amounts of cash in the process.

In recent years, the case of Paul Merson only serves to underline the power of an addiction to gambling. In November 1994, Merson admitted that he was addicted to cocaine, alcohol and gambling. At a sensational press conference, he announced, 'I am a gambling addict and have to face the fact that there is no cure. I was losing more on the horses than my mum and dad would have earned from a year of hard work.'

He spent six weeks in an addiction clinic, with the backing of his club and the FA, and later broke down in tears at an emotional press conference when he announced that he was receiving treatment for his triple addiction. He admitted that he was having problems in his relationship with his wife, Lorraine, with the trio of addiction clinics – Alcoholics Anonymous, Narcotics Anonymous and Gamblers Anonymous – beginning to take their toll. Discussing his predicament with fellow addicts at his group meetings had become crucial to him. 'It's an awful thing to say,' he said, 'but I find it easier to talk about my problems with them than with my wife. The meetings are where I bare my soul and get all my feelings out in the open, not at home. I don't blame Lorraine for being fed up of me. I just go to the group therapy meetings, come home, watch telly, go to the meetings, come home, watch telly, watch more telly – and that is no life for Lorraine.'

Things took a turn for the better for Merson in June 1997 when he remarried Lorraine in a sunset ceremony in the courtyard of the five-star Sandy Lane Hotel in Barbados. Arsenal team-mate David Platt was best man, and Gianluca Vialli was one of just six friends invited to the wedding. Merson's recovery from his addiction has been admirable and today he is playing the best football of his career with Middlesbrough. Without finding courage to face up to his problems things could have turned out very differently. In October 1990, Merson told the *News of the World*, 'I've blown £100,000 in betting shops. And it wasn't only the gee-gees. I'd bet on anything – football, snooker, dogs, cricket, even bowls'.

Merson says gambling was the main factor in his descent into drug dependence and his debts fluctuated between a minimum of £150,000 to a high of around £400,000. Former West Ham and England star Trevor Brooking offers an insight into why footballers are so prone to gambling and in the worst-case scenario, a serious addiction. 'An obvious answer is that they earn larger amounts of money much earlier than most youngsters who may be entering longer term professions,' says Brooking. 'This extra bit of spending power can certainly tempt them into squandering wages as they enjoy this new, apparent wealth. Another point is the amount of spare time young players have. Most training days don't extend much beyond lunchtime and so, unless young players are encouraged to continue with some form of further education, those long empty afternoons see them drifting down to the betting shop or watching the horse racing or other sports on television.

'At nearly every club there is a handful of keen betting enthusiasts who bring in the racing newspapers and study form each day. They can influence the younsters. Another factor is that footballers travel to meetings and events where naturally they come into contact with influential connections within the different sports. Not surprisingly, the players receive tips and useful snippets of information which convince them it's worth placing a large bet on certain races.'

Trevor Brooking was in charge of providing cards for the card schools on West Ham away trips in the 1970s. Many players had their introduction to gambling on such journeys. 'Card schools at football clubs are another potentially dangerous area in which debts can develop. Teams travel all over the country and hours and hours are spent on coaches. To dispel the boredom, footballers play a variety of games. I used to be a participant. Most games were recreational with just small stakes involved but there were the odd sessions where brag, shoot, pontoon and poker were introduced, and that was when the stakes could get out of hand. These games tend to bring out the true gambler and unfortunately it can lead to the stupid situation where a player can lose heavily. It's hardly the ideal preparation for him to turn in a peak performance on the pitch.'

Northern Ireland international Keith Gillespie is another modern-day star who nearly gambled his way to oblivion. In February 1996 the tabloids revealed that Gillespie had gone on a £62,000 gambling spree, which included losing £47,000 in one day. Gillespie's gambling habit was fuelled by his £5,000 a week wages and he did a lot of it over the telephone. He dug himself into a deep hole by frantically attempting to recoup his mounting losses, and ended up being chased for the cash by an angry bookmaker. His problems began when he backed a string of losers over four consecutive days which cost him £15,000. By the Friday he began to panic and decided to go for a couple of big bets to try and put himself back in credit. He rang Mickey Arnott, who ran S. Prices Bookmakers in Newcastle, and won £833 betting £1,000 on a favourite at Newmarket. After that initial bit of luck, it all started to go wrong for Gillespie as he backed loser after loser. He bet £2,000 each way on a horse which was running for the first time, £4,000 on the 5/2 favourite Innocent George which came in sixth at Bangor, and made wildly optimistic bets on evening greyhound races at Oxford, Sunderland and Menmore.

Gillespie met his Waterloo when a £20,000 cheque he had

given to S. Prices to clear some of his debts bounced. He decided to confess his problems to Newcastle's then manager, Kevin Keegan. Rather charitably, Keegan arranged for the club to settle the debt, with the player paying the club back out of his match bonuses, on the condition that he stopped gambling 'crazy money'.

Gillespie remembers well the day he hit his rock bottom. 'It was a mad day – I was just chasing a winner. I haven't a clue how many races I bet on. I just bet on every single one. I kept thinking, My luck must change, but it didn't. I just sat there on the phone. I didn't even keep a note of how much I was spending. I had a rough idea, but I never really knew. I thought that if I had just one win I would be able to wipe the slate clean. But when I look back I think if I had won I would still be betting today. It sounds silly, but it's probably lucky for me I didn't win.'

Keith Gillespie started betting at an early age when he was a seventeen year old on Manchester United's books. His gambling only became a serious problem when he moved to Newcastle as the £1 million makeweight in Andy Cole's £7 million move in the opposite direction. 'I went from wages on a moderate scale to high wages,' Gillespie recalls. 'Money seemed to come to me overnight. I was just betting out of boredom. When I first started in the bookies I'd put a tenner or maybe £50 on. But when I did it on the phone I'd put more on. I started upping the betting to a couple of hundred quid, then £500 and eventually a grand or more. It seems much easier when you're saying numbers over the phone rather than handing the cash over.'

Keith Gillespie's father, Harry, a prison officer at Belfast's Maze Prison, was deeply concerned about his son. 'I'm staggered,' he said at the time. 'The most I've seen him bet was a fiver. We'd pick four horses for a 40p yankee multiple bet costing £4.48. That's the most I've ever seen him gamble – I thought he had more sense. I don't know whether all the money has gone to his head but how can he throw it all away? I fear he may need help.'

Few would have argued with Gillespie Senior's view. 'In fact, one of Gillespie's friends, quoted anonymously in the press, referred to him as a classic 'mug punter' who 'was playing with professional gamblers' stakes but had no idea what he was doing'. In September 1996, Gillespie announced in the *Sun*, 'I'll never bet again. The fact that I owed this money had been hanging over me. I couldn't sleep. I was too deep. But when it came out in the paper I was glad, it was a relief. It made me see sense at last.' Gillespie also paid tribute to Newcastle fans for refusing to condemn him. 'I was worried what they'd say because the fans save hard for the season tickets and there was me blowing loads of cash. But they were great. People said to me, "It's your money, do what you like with it." '

Unsurprisingly, Gillespie didn't escape the dressing-room banter, with Robert Lee announcing in the Christmas edition of Newcastle's *Black and White* magazine that he would be giving Gillespie a copy of the life story of Peter O'Sullivan so that the winger could learn what a real racing expert is.

Gillespie doesn't gamble at all now and puts his kicking of the habit down to playing golf and going shopping in Newcastle with his flatmate – plus a touch of fear, no doubt.

Former England goalkeeper Peter Shilton has rightly earned his place in football's hall of fame. A super-fit, athletic and naturally talented player, Shilton is very much a member of the 'Been there, seen it, done it club'. Shilton was once Britain's highest-paid player, earning an estimated

£250,000 a year, and it was during this period that he succumbed to a gambling addiction. One joke goes that upon returning to his home after a day at the races and a few drinks, Shilton waltzed into his bedroom and asked his wife what time it was. 'Ten to one,' she replied. 'Oh, I'll have £40 each way,' said Shilts. It's a good story but the reality is that gambling addicts will bet on anything. At the height of his playing and earning power in the late 1980s, Shilton owned three luxury houses and bred racehorses. In the following year, it all started to go wrong, culminating in a court appearance in October 1995 when he faced debts of over £450,000. One of his creditors was the Professional Footballers Association, who had provided him with secret loans over a number of years. Most of his financial problems stemmed from his gambling addiction and aside from the PFA, six banks and building societies joined the queue of creditors. Shilton was facing financial ruin.

He suggested a compromise deal whereby he would pay off the cash he owed at so much in the pound, but the PFA were given legal advice that it couldn't be accepted because of their responsibility to their 2,000 members. It was revealed that his most recent loan from the PFA was for £20,000, secured by his pension rights. PFA chairman, Gordon Taylor, commented, 'It's sad to see a leading personality in the game in this situation. Nobody can accuse us of not helping Peter down the years. But there must be a limit. The monies loaned were based on a commitment to repay them. I'm not in a position to waive that commitment.'

Fortunately for Shilton, he escaped being declared bankrupt when his creditors accepted his plan to pay off his debts. No details were disclosed but it was generally thought that Shilton had offered to pay 22p in every pound that he earned to his creditors. 'This agreement will enable me to arrange my finances to the benefit of all concerned,' said Shilton. 'I am also grateful to my creditors for their understanding and co-operation. I look forward to the future with great confidence. I believe I have a lot to offer football in the future. I would like to take up the promotional side of the game.'

By December 1996 Shilton was penniless and living in a rented house in Coventry. He had been destroyed by his hopeless addiction to gambling, forcing him to put his retirement from the game on hold. He made his 100th League appearance in December 1996 playing for Leyton Orient. He kept a clean sheet in a 2-0 victory over Brighton.

To be fair to Peter Shilton, he was unlucky in property matters which contributed to his debts. The property slump of the early 1990s left Shilton and his wife Sue with negative equity on three houses, prompting him to gamble even more than usual to try and recoup some of his lost property values. Sue Shilton was blissfully unaware of her husband's mounting financial problems but her suspicions were aroused when she had to sell her Mini (a Christmas present from Peter) and exchange it for a bike. 'I knew nothing about many of the financial problems,' said Sue. 'When I found out I felt this anger towards him.'

In January 1995 his Southampton home was repossessed and sold by a building society. Just a few months before, in October 1994, his assistant at Plymouth Argyle, John McGovern, walked out claiming that Shilton owed him £7,000. Two months later, racehorse trainer Martin Pipe began a bankruptcy petition against Shilton in order to retrieve £3,000 he was owed for the training of two horses. Early in 1995, Shilton resigned as manager of Plymouth, a week after having been suspended by the club for failing to repay them £5,000.

It is sad that Peter Shilton's exemplary playing career has been counterbalanced by his gambling problems. His long-time friend and biographer, James Thomas, describes Shilton thus: 'Sometimes I think he's a little demented, a very difficult but fascinating man. He never does anything by halves whether it's goalkeeping, gambling – where he has taken ridiculous risks – or drinking, where he has thought nothing of going on a two-day bender.' But that's another story.

There are footballers who gamble – and then there's Steve Claridge. In his autobiography, *Tales from the Boot Camps*, Claridge reveals that he gambled away his £500 football apprenticeship fee in just one afternoon. His book is a full and frank account of his gambles both on and off the pitch. He confesses to frittering away over £300,000 on bets and being addicted to gambling for fifteen years. Such was his obsession with gambling that he even worked behind the counter at a bookmakers office for a while. When he eventually fell on hard times, he squatted in the flat of one of the directors of Aldershot FC to make ends meet. Claridge once drove into the back of a lorry while trying to get to a betting shop on time and he even borrowed money from trainers to fuel his habit. Currently 'in remission', Claridge was still gambling as recently as the spring of 1997. He admitted to the *Daily Sport*: 'I grabbed a bit of the 7/2 available on Leicester City [his club] before the Coca-Cola Cup semi-final against Wimbledon. I'm not going to tell you how much I've had on, but it will be a very nice little pick-up if I win,' said Claridge.

Leicester City not only won that semi-final but went on to

win the final as well, with Steve Claridge scoring the winning goal in the replay. He was much in demand for interviews and revealed to a group of journalists that he had also had a bet at 1/2 on Manchester United to win the FA Carling Premiership title. Eyebrows were raised because Leicester City still had to play against United and Claridge was ordered by the FA to call off his bet. FA spokesman Steve Double explained what had happened: 'The Premier League received a complaint about Steve Claridge from a member of the public [reportedly a fan of Manchester United's Championship rivals, Liverpool]. They pased it on to us, and Claridge was immediately informed that he had to call off the bet.'

Claridge did what he was told, saying, 'I accept what the FA tell me. It wasn't a massive wager. I stood to pocket hundreds of pounds rather than thousands.' If Claridge had not mentioned the bet to journalists, none would have been any the wiser.

The Football Authorities and the betting industry remain vigilant in policing the specific betting rules for players and officials. The FA voiced concern in the autumn of 1994 over a 'first to score bet' placed by three Liverpool players ahead of their Coca-Cola Cup match against Burnley. Neil Ruddock, Steve McManaman and Jamie Redknapp backed team-mate John Scales to score the game's first goal at odds of 33/1. He did, and the players reportedly pocketed £330 for their £10 stake. Immediately, the FA wrote to Liverpool asking for their observations. In fact, it was not the first time that John Scales had won his team-mates some money. In the January of 1994, the *Sunday Express* reported that Vinnie Jones won £2,000, and the rest of the Wimbledon team won a total of £2,000, when Scales scored in the third minute of a match against Sunderland. 'The odds of 40/1 were too good to ignore,' said Scales, 'and I encouraged some of the others to have a flutter. I fancied myself to score from a setpiece and luckily the chance came early on.'

Players betting on team-mates is dangerous territory but it can also mean big money. In December 1992, Colchester United players clubbed together to put £200 on defender Martin Granger, at odds of 20/1, to score the first goal in a home game against Northampton. Colchester were awarded a penalty and supporters expected Colchester's normal penalty taker, Roy McDonough, to do the honours. Instead, up stepped Granger to slot the ball home – winning his team-mates £4,000. 'We just took advantage of inside knowledge,' said one player at the time. How convenient.

On the other hand, Chelsea captain Dennis Wise turned down the chance to win £560 when the Blues were awarded a penalty in an end-of-season match against Wimbledon in April 1993. Wise and Chelsea striker Tony Cascarino had both backed young midfielder Damian Matthew with £20 at odds of 28/1 to score the game's first goal. When Chelsea were awarded a penalty Wise (Chelsea's regular penalty taker at the time) initially handed the ball to Matthew, but then changed his mind and decided to take it himself. Wise remembers, 'Cas was not happy, but I knew I couldn't really let him take it.'

Republic of Ireland international striker Tony Cascarino may not have been impressed by Dennis Wise's actions but the money they could have won was chicken feed compared with the sort of wagers he has made during his gambling career. Cascarino puts years of disappointing form down to his addiction to gambling. He bet on football, horses, dogs and predominantly poker. He told the *News of the World* in a revealing interview that he frequented south London gambling dens and once had a shotgun pushed into his face when a group of gangsters raided his game. He admitted, 'I have let the best years of my career slip away from me by not giving one hundred per cent. The word was out not to touch me with a bargepole. Gambling became more important to me than football.'

One bet that Cascarino remembers well is one that would have netted him £100,000. Coventry scored a late equaliser to deny him eight out of eight predictions in a football accumulator. After quitting the English game, Cascarino plied his trade in France with Marseille, a city not known for a betting shop on every corner.

Stan Bowles was one of the most gifted footballers of his generation and on a few occasions he was chosen to represent England. He could have gambled for England too. Bowles freely admits to years of gambling, especially on horses, and found it easy to cope with his job and his addiction. 'I seemed to be able to move between the football world and the underworld as easily as if I was stepping from one room to another,' said Bowles. Indeed, most of his gambling life was perfectly straighforward, although in the 1960s he was rumoured to be loosely connected with the very dodgy Quality Street Gang, who tricked Manchester bookmakers out of thousands of pounds.

Looking back on his career, Bowles openly admits that he played football so that he could gamble, rather than being a footballer who liked a flutter. 'If I didn't play football I had no money. If I didn't have any money I couldn't gamble,' says Bowles.

His biggest loss was £57,000 in just four months, and he claims to have won and lost £1 million during his gambling career. His biggest loss in one day was £15,000, while his biggest single win totalled £18,000. Playing football was light relief from the pressures of gambling, although even when he was on the field he tried to keep in touch with his bets. 'Those ninety minutes were a relief to me,' said Bowles. 'I could get away from it. It was a bit of fun. If I'd had a bet I'd just make sure I was over the far side and get near somebody with a radio to find out what had won.'

Former Crewe manager Ernie Tagg once said of Stan Bowles, 'If he could pass a betting shop as well as he could pass the ball, he wouldn't have had a problem.'

Of course, it wasn't all plain sailing and the pitfalls of gambling became all too apparent to Bowles. 'I went skint two or three times and my marriage broke up,' remembers Bowles, 'but I still managed eighteen years in the professional game.'

His eagerly awaited autobiography, *Stan the Man*, was published in 1997 and recounts numerous tales of his gambling with the notorious Quality Street Gang and a character called Carlisle Peter. Bowles started betting at a very early age; he was only thirteen when he started running bets for drinks in his local pub by running back and forth to the betting shop on the regulars' behalf.

Bowles's natural talent allowed many a blind eye to be turned to his unorthodox antics. In the 1970s he was the creative engine room of a great Queens Park Rangers side which included Rodney Marsh and Gerry Francis. He was worshipped by the Rangers fans but was a source of great irritation to his manager Dave Sexton. He used to turn up on match days just fifteen minutes before kickoff because he didn't want to be bored by a long talk about team tactics. Such was his natural charisma that on one occasion he managed to persuade Sexton to take a full-strength QPR team to play a pre-season friendly against Ford Open Prison where one of his friends was spending time at Her Majesty's pleasure.

On another occasion Bowles's antics landed him in a Belgian jail along with his QPR team-mate Don Shanks. The pair arrived back at the team hotel at 3 a.m. hoping to get another drink, only to find the bar closed. Don Shanks bet Bowles £10 that he could get another drink from the night porter by collapsing on the floor and pretending that he was ill. Shanks fell to the floor and Bowles demanded a large brandy to 'revive the patient'. Shanks drank the brandy down in one, jumped up, handed the waiter the empty glass, thanked him very much and said goodnight. Laughing, the two players headed for bed as the waiter looked on in amazement.

A quarter of an hour later, Bowles was awoken by the sound of a commotion outside including the noise of excitable-sounding dogs. All of a sudden there was a pounding on his hotel room door. The police arrested Bowles and Shanks and swiftly hauled them off to the local station, where they were roughed up and left to spend the rest of the night in the cells. The following morning, they were sent on their way after being told the reason for their arrest: in Belgium, it was considered a serious offence to make a hoax call for an ambulance, which is what the hotel night porter had done when he saw Shanks collapse on the floor!

Another oddball Bowles bet almost started a crowd riot at Sunderland. It was the last game of the 1973 season and Second Division Sunderland were celebrating their famous FA Cup Final victory over Leeds United. The club had set up a trestle table alongside the pitch on which the FA Cup would be displayed to the ecstatic Sunderland fans. Stan Bowles, while appreciating the occasion, was more interested in winning the £10 bet he had made with one of his old Carlisle mates (he played for Carlisle United before he went to QPR) – that he could knock the FA Cup trophy off its perch the first time he got the ball.

Soon after the kickoff, the ball found its way to Bowles, who clearly remembers what happened next. 'I tore off straight across the park. Everyone on the pitch was just staring at me – and then, bang! The FA Cup goes shooting up in the air. The whole ground knew that I had done it on purpose – then the Sunderland fans went ape. They wanted my bollocks in their sandwiches.' Bowles then provoked a major pitch invasion by pretending to be headbutted by Micky Horswill, an incident which led to the Sunderland player being sent off. 'At least I got my tenner,' said Bowles.

Once a gambler, always a gambler. Stan Bowles's gambling addiction was so strong that even when he joined Gamblers Anonymous he ended up betting how long he would stay with the group. Today, Bowles helps out with some occasional youth coaching and no longer gambles to the levels that he once did – probably due to the fact that he simply hasn't got the available funds to do so. He may have lost a fortune, but no-one can ever deny that he was one of English football's shining lights.

Inevitably, greed has been the downfall of many players, not least ex-pro Jimmy Gauld, who was the criminal mastermind behind this century's biggest sporting scandal. Gauld set up a match-fixing ring that saw England internationals Tony Kay and Peter Swan imprisoned for four months after they bet on their Sheffield Wednesday side being beaten by Ipswich Town. The players were gullible pawns in a scheme that netted Gauld as much as £1,000 a week. It was also claimed that he masterminded the throwing of fourteen games. It was only when Bristol Rovers goalkeeper, Esmond Million, conceded two goals in a manner so suspicious it had to be a fix that the FA and the police brought Gauld's world crashing down. He was sentenced to four years in prison for his misdemeanours.

Much more recently, in 1990 Lou Macari, the then manager of Swindon Town, was fined £1,000 for his part in a betting scandal after a bet of £6,500 was placed on Swindon to lose a Cup match against Newcastle. Lou Macari maintained his innocence, telling reporters, 'When you are innocent, even the fine of one penny would have been a penny too much.' All very well but at one point Macari faced the very real possibility of a jail term, forcing his wife to ring round friends to collect her husband's bail money of £50,000.

Lou Macari had been a known gambler, having frequented the bookies since his early days at Celtic. One Swindon bookmaker reveals, 'Lou was a regular visitor but in the end I asked him not to bet with me any more because of the size and frequency of his bets. On one occasion he emptied his pockets while in my place. I cleaned up his used betting slips and there was £800 worth.'

Given that the Scots like a flutter as much as anyone else, it's hardly surprising that Glasgow Rangers manager Walter Smith banned all his players in 1991 from travelling to Cheltenham for the annual festival of racing. Ally McCoist decided to go anyway and amazingly, as he has a reputation for being very difficult to locate, was found out and dropped from a vital Old Firm derby for ignoring the manager's orders.

Above board or not, the temptation to bet on football is often just too great. Stevenage Borough chairman Victor Green won £25,000 when his team won the Vauxhall Conference in 1996. He bet £1,000 at odds of 25-1 with William Hill that his team would take the title and was rewarded with the biggest ever pay-out for a winning bet on non-League football. Some compensation, then, for the fact that Stevenage were denied promotion to the Third Division because their ground did not meet the Football League standards.

In the same season, Gillingham chairman P. D. Scally nearly won £20,000 when he registered as a player with the intention of playing in the final few minutes of the Gils' last home game of the seaon against Scarborough. Scally explained his bet. 'It was a private bet with the managing director of a company called Sarkpoint Reprographics Ltd, who put up a wager of £20,000 on the basis that I play at least ten minutes in a football League game for Gillingham before the season ended. To achieve this, I needed to register as a player before the transfer deadline on the last Thursday of March and then convince my manager to select me for the final game at Priestfield Stadium, at home to Scarborough.'

However, all did not go according to plan and Scally had to admit defeat. 'Unfortunately, due to political reasons, it was difficult for me to take the place of a player who had played all season, or been involved in the squad, but none the less the decision was left to me on the day. I was unable to justify going on and of course it would have been a huge stigma for a player to have been replaced by the 40-year-old chairman of his football club and therefore I didn't achieve the bet,' laments Scally. Who said all football chairmen were self-centred egomaniacs?

One man at the front of the queue when God was handing out egos is Michael Knighton, a man with his heart in the right place who at best could be described as headstrong. In 1989, a 38-year-old man turned up in Graham Sharpe's William Hill office (Sharpe is now the PR guru and public face of William Hill) asking for odds on the bet that he would play First Division football at some time during the following season, 1989/90. He said that he had played a few games for a professional club at junior level before his career was ended by injury. He also explained to Sharpe that his wife was about to publish a book about the power of self-belief and the benefits of a new diet, and that he intended to promote the book by getting fit and betting on himself to play at the highest level.

He wanted to bet an amount that, if successful, would win him a lump sum of well into six figures. Totally unaware of Knighton's identity, Sharpe felt sure that it was pretty well impossible for the 'mystery visitor' to achieve his aim and was ready to offer him odds of 20,000/1 with a maximum stake of £50, which would give Knighton winnings of £1 million.

The following day, Graham Sharpe picked up a copy of the *Sun*, turned to the sports pages, and saw a picture of Michael Knighton, who was planning to buy Manchester United Football Club. Knighton telephoned Sharpe some days later and said that had he accepted the bet, he would have insisted on Alex Ferguson playing him as substitute in an end-of-season match so that he could have cleaned up. As it happens, Knighton's plan to buy Manchester United never really took off – and would Alex Ferguson really have left McClair on the bench for a man playing out his egotistical fantasies?

Blind faith often plays its part in 'inside' football bets. When Peterborough United were relegated from the Third Division at the end of season 1996/97, manager Barry Fry revealed that he had backed his team to win the Championship. 'I put my money where my mouth is – £12,000,' he told the *Sport*. 'I had £5,000 each way and then after we lost our first game I went out and had another couple of grand on it.'

When Dave Bassett was the manager of Sheffield United Football Club, he chose an unsual way to motivate his players. In February 1993, he bet his players £500 that they would lose in a match against Oldham Athletic. Stung by this lack of managerial confidence, the Blades won comfortably, leaving Bassett 'delighted' to cough up their winnings. A shrewd bit of psychology, if nothing else.

For unusual bets, look no further than goalkeepers. The unorthodox Bruce Grobbelaar once walked the length of Wembley Stadium on his hands to win a cash bet. At the end of the 1899/1900 season, Burnley's sixteen stone, six foot goalkeeper, Jack Hillman, won a bet by keeping a clean sheet in a charity match with one hand tied behind his back. Legendary hardman Dave Mackay once won £80 from his Tottenham team-mates when he ate a bouquet of flowers.

Ex-international and Liverpool defender turned TV pundit Alan Hansen preyed on the betting habits of footballers in 1991. Kenny Dalglish had just resigned as Liverpool manager and Hansen called the team into the dressing room to announce that he was the new boss. Hansen's performance was so convincing, a number of senior players allegedly dashed straight to the local bookies to put money on Hansen becoming the next Liverpool manager. The odds immediately shifted from 7/2 to 7/4, installing Hansen as the bookies' favourite for the job. Later the same afternoon, Alan Hansen admitted that his 'appointment' had been a windup, much to the annoyance of the players who had backed him.

Atlantic City and Las Vegas aside, on the face of it gambling seems to be a very British disease. How many times have you seen a betting shop on the corner of some foreign street? It is true to say that foreign players in general do not share the British penchant for gambling but one or two have enjoyed a flutter from time to time.

In January 1997, the Sporting Gijon players won £40,000 on Spain's state-run football lottery game by correctly predicting the outcome of most of the fifteen games on the list. One of the fixtures they got right was their own game against rivals Oviedo, which they predicted would either end in a draw or a win for Oviedo. A week after the match, the Spanish Football Federation announced that they would not be taking action against the players, despite the obvious eyebrow raising over the prediction and result.

A barman at a Spanish tennis club was convinced that his luck was in when he correctly predicted the outcome of thirteen matches listed on the *Quiniela* (Spanish football lottery coupon) out of a list of fourteen matches. The final match on his coupon was the Barcelona v. Valencia fixture on a Monday night early in 1998. The barman stood to win a share in the jackpot if the match ended as either a home win or a draw. Barcelona cruised into a 3-0 lead halfway through the second half and, feeling that he had seen enough, the barman popped down to the cellar to find a vintage bottle of champagne. By the time he re-emerged from the cellar, Valencia had pulled a couple of goals back, but the barman's confidence was still high.

Two minutes from the end of the game, Ortega equalised for Valencia before grabbing the winner for the away team. The po-faced barman was left trying to put the cork back into the champagne bottle.

German football was stunned by a betting story in June 1997. In his *Secret Diaries*, former German captain Lothar Matthaus revealed that he had bet Bayern Munich's general manager Uli Hoeness £3,000 that Jurgen Klinsmann would not score fifteen goals in the season that had just finished. A few days after the book was published, Matthaus was stripped of the captaincy of Bayern Munich for his indiscretion. To make matters worse, he lost the bet too, because Klinsmann scored fifteen goals exactly, helping Bayern win their record fourteenth German Bundesliga title.

Klinsmann and Matthaus made no secret of their mutual dislike while playing together at Bayern. Klinsmann commented after the bet was made public, 'There are much better ways of spending so much money than making bets against a team-mate. I just can't take Matthaus seriously now.'

Matthaus tried to smooth things over by saying, 'It was the first bet I was glad to lose because I knew that if Klinsmann scored fifteen goals, we would be champions.'

If you fancy winning serious amounts of money gambling on the outcome of football matches, try and get chummy with the Thai businessman who in October 1994 took his bookies to the cleaners. Clearly a man of some considerable financial means, he bet £286,000 on six matches and made £410,000. He began with an £80,000 bet on Nottingham Forest to beat Wimbledon and won £122,666 – the biggest ever win on a bet on League football. The next day he turned the bookies over again with a £10,000 wager on Boavista of

Portugal to beat Napoli and £37,500 on Newcastle United to beat Atletico Bilbao in their European clash. Talk about a lucky run. In the same week he picked up £137,500 when Bayern Leverkusen beat Honved and £113,000 when Gothenburg got the better of Galatasaray in the Champions' League.

For the millions of sensible bets that are placed in a year, there are a few inevitably odd ones as well. In July 1993, the editor of a Sheffield Wednesday fanzine placed a £5 bet at a million to one odds. The bet was made up of five different parts:

1   That the Archbishop of Canterbury would confirm a second coming before August 1996.
2   That Jesus Christ (in his new incarnation) would play for Sheffield Wednesday by the time he was twenty.
3   That Jesus Christ would be named Footballer of the Year before the age of twenty.
4   That he would play for England before his twentieth birthday.
5   That Sheffield United would manage to avoid relegation in the 1993/94 season.

Even if conditions 1–4 were met, the bet was ruined by condition 5 when Sheffield United were relegated on the last day of the season.

In 1991, a Newcastle United fan bet William Hill £10 at odds of 1,000/1 that his wife would have a baby on the same day as Newcastle played in the FA Cup Final. He lost the bet on both counts because Newcastle were knocked out of the Cup by Nottingham Forest in the fourth round and his wife failed to give birth on Cup Final day.

For some reason, optimism just surges through a punter's

veins – perhaps none more so than in the Reading postman who bet £5 that Mr Blobby would replace ousted England manager Graham Taylor. At odds of 50,000/1 it was a long shot, but to the gambler some things are irresistible.

Knowing the game inside out, so the theory goes, is the only realistic way to score a major victory over the bookies and some betting successes seem to confirm this. At the beginning of the 1992/93 season, Jim Wright, a 57-year-old coach company employee from Teignmouth, placed a £1,000 each-way treble predicting that Newcastle United would win the First Division title at odds of 8/1, Stoke City would win Division Two at 6/1 and Cardiff City would win Division Three at odds of 9/1. He won £654,375 and maintained his sense of humour when he told the press, 'I'm determined not to invest the money wisely.' It was the first time a customer had total winnings that smashed through Ladbroke's £500,000 win limit.

Large sums of money do not necessarily have to be wagered to achieve extraordinary gambling success. Two friends, Tom Davis and Phil Korny, from Clitheroe in Lancashire, placed a joint £1 accumulator bet on the outcome of fourteen football matches in October 1987. Thirteen of the games bet upon came up on the Saturday afternoon, leaving the last match in the accumulator to be played on the Sunday. It was the Scottish Skol Cup Final between Rangers and Aberdeen. The two men tipped a draw, but with five minutes of the game remaining, Rangers were losing. With just a couple of minutes to go, they equalised and Davis and Korny pocketed the biggest ever pay-out on an accumulator bet, totalling £397,726.99.

It was a record that stood for nearly ten years before it was broken by 56-year-old Graham Jenkins from Bournemouth. Jenkins invested £10 of his hard-earned money on a fifteen-match accumulator at the bookies on Saturday 25 June 1997. The unique thing about the bet was that Jenkins did not bother studying the fixtures in detail and spent all of 30 seconds filling in the coupon.

The bet ran into some problems early on when one of the games was postponed due to bad weather and another was abandoned. Jenkins was then left with thirteen matches in his accumulator – twelve on Saturday and one on Monday evening. His eight home victories and four away victories predicted for the Saturday matches all came up and he knew that he was due to pick up a minimum of £117,000 if the Monday night result went his way – Raith Rovers winning away at Airdrie in the Scottish Tennents Cup. The odds were 11/5. Instead of going to the game or sitting at home listening to the radio, Jenkins went to bed early because he had to get up for work the following morning.

The match was eventually won by Raith 4-1 but only after they conceded an early goal. Cool as a cucumber, Jenkins only found out about his record-breaking win when he looked for the match result in his morning newspaper. A lucky punter if ever there was one. The odds of achieving a second win by guessing all the results correctly would be millions to one.

Being a clued-up punter is often half the battle but one thing the bookmakers do not like is being outsmarted. In April 1996, Torquay United were nine points adrift at the foot of Division Three. A man popped into his local branch of Joe Jennings and asked for odds that Torquay would not be relegated. He was given 33/1 and placed £42, giving himself potential winnings of £1,428. What the bookmakers were unaware of was that Torquay United would only be relegated to the Vauxhall Conference League if the winners of that division had facilities deemed appropriate for full Football League status. Stevenage Borough were massively ahead at the top of the Vauxhall Conference and the punter knew that their facilities were not up to scratch. Torquay finished bottom of Division Three but avoided relegation by default.

The punter won his money but Joe Jennings were not exactly gracious in defeat. A spokesman said: 'It's a small-time coup and we'll pay out. But there's a principle here. The lack of integrity is what disturbs us. The punter had information that we didn't have before placing the bet.'

Before the arrival of the National Lottery, the football pools were the first real way that large masses of the population could gamble on the same sporting event. People from all walks of life 'did the pools', including royalty. A royal insider revealed to Andrew Morton, author of *Diana: Her True Story*, that the Duke of Edinburgh is a keen pools punter. The duke, it was claimed, sits in front of the television on a Saturday evening checking his coupon. 'People will wonder if he puts a cross for no publicity,' said the insider.

As we are all aware, money can bring out the worst in people. Four workmates who formed a pools syndicate in 1990 verbally agreed that if one member of the syndicate won more than £1 million the other three would receive £25,000 each. Paul Pitt, one of the syndicate, won £1.8 million and also gained a selective memory. The 28-year-old millionaire celebrated his win by buying a round of drinks for his syndicate colleagues but didn't give them a penny. Furious, the other three started legal proceedings and the case reached court in 1995. Pitt was sued for breach of contract and lost the case. The judge ruled that he should pay each of the remaining syndicate members £25,000 each, plus £14,000 interest and up to £80,000 in legal fees.

To win the pools once is a monumental stroke of good luck but to win the jackpot twice has only ever happened once. In 1969, Matt Clarke from Cleveleys, Lancashire, won £778,426 on Vernons Pools. Just when the winnings had almost run out, he won again in August 1993 and landed a £750,000 payout.

In recent years, it's the major tournaments that have attracted widespread betting by football lovers and non-football lovers alike. During the 1990 World Cup punters bet millions and the tournament produced Britain's first £1 million punter, who ended a two-week spree with a profit of £18,000. At one stage, the gambler, who was a London-based foreigner, was £500,000 down to William Hill after losing a series of big bets including £100,000 on West Germany to beat England in the semi-final in 90 minutes and £60,000 on Italy to beat Argentina, which they didn't. He came back from the dead by winning £210,000 when Italy beat England in the third-place play-off match and won a further £48,000 when West Germany beat Argentina in the final 1-0.

In Britain, up to £60 million was gambled on the 1994 World Cup finals. Some of the biggest punters were overseas clients of the bookmakers – one Australian William Hill customer laid out total bets of £428,000 and ended up £100,000 down at the end of the competition. The calmest person watching the final was almost certainly Harold Anand, a 56-year-old clerk from north London who stood to win £124,000 if Italy won the cup and £106,000 if Brazil won it, having staked two £400 accumulator bets in August

1993. This meant he had £17,700 riding on Italy at 6/1 and the same amount on Brazil at 5/1.

The tournament's single biggest loser was a Malaysian who bet £121,000 on Mexico to beat Bulgaria and exactly the same amount on Brazil to beat Italy in the final within 90 minutes – neither bet came off. On the other hand, the single biggest winner was a Hong Kong restaurant owner who won £165,000 when Brazil beat Sweden. Perhaps the most optimistic wager of the tournament was placed by Essex lorry driver Tony Tedwell, who put £400 on Ireland to win the World Cup Final 3-0, against any opposition, at odds of 200-1.

The Cameroon v. Russia match attracted a lot of attention from the gambling fraternity when a rumour spread that the Russians would not be trying very hard as they were already virtually out of the tournament. Money poured into the bookmakers from all over the world, nearly all of it on Cameroon to win. Odds dived from odds against to odds on, with one punter betting £10,000 on a 3-0 win for the Lions of Cameroon. The bookies breathed a huge sigh of relief when the Russians ended up 6-1 winners. Oleg Salenko smashed the most-goals-scored-in-one-World-Cup-match record, netting five goals in total. Just think what the odds for that feat would have been.

The early Draconian rules of betting on football matches are an eternity away from today's sophisticated industry. The levy of the betting tax raises millions and millions of pounds for the Treasury as the industry enjoys an unprecedented high. Even so, the FA have historically been hostile to the betting industry. Rule 26 (a) (vi) of Lancaster Gate's Law Book states clearly that anybody connected with bookmaking is barred from having anything to do with the game – whether as a director, player, referee or any kind of official. Graham Sharpe, the public face of William Hill, is not a fan of the rule. He is a director of Wealdstone FC, chairman of a Sunday League club and, through William Hill, a sponsor of numerous footballing causes. Sharpe says, 'It seems to me to be completely wrong that, strictly speaking, I am barred from being involved in football, yet they would be happy to roll out the welcome mat for any murderer or common criminal who fancied being the director of a football club.'

Football is certainly guilty of hypocrisy where the betting industry is concerned. 'The FA have done everything in their power to stifle it,' says Sharpe. 'Then on the other hand, they are perfectly happy to accept money from bookmakers.' Ladbrokes were one of the major sponsors of Euro 96. The gambling industry's critics argue that football needs protection from bookmakers because of the real danger of match fixing. The betting industry dismisses such accusations as out of hand, stating that considering the number of games played under strict organisation and rules, the percentage proved to have been manipulated, rigged or fixed is microscopic. Anyway, bookmakers would stand to lose too if match fixing was rife.

The fun of a bet, however occasional, is something that millions of people enjoy. For the addicted, the consequences can be serious – financial ruin, broken marriages and ruined careers. The players who have gambled 'big' have lost thousands but at least, in most cases, they have been able to salvage some sort of life by jumping on the football gravy train again. Talent on the pitch has rarely been affected by this compulsive habit. But however tempting big-money gambling may seem, remember one crucial thing: you never see a poor bookie.

6 The World

QUESTION: What is worse than being the manager of Manchester City? Answer: Being a member of Iraq's national team – but only just.

In their quest to reach the 1998 World Cup finals in France, the Iraqi national team certainly had more downs than ups. Halfway through 1997, Iraq's World Cup dream ended when they lost at home to Kazakhstan, a result which did not please Uday Hussein, head of the Iraq Football Federation and son of Saddam. After the match, a deranged Hussein Jnr sacked the manager and carted the team off to the sinister Radwaniyah military base, 35 miles from Baghdad, to be whipped and beaten on the soles of their feet. Call me old-fashioned, but in my book this was hardly the ideal preparation for their next game. There were even reports that the players had been executed by firing squad on the specific orders of Hussein, a man who makes Attila the Hun look like McCaulay Culkin. Little concrete evidence was found to support this story although it has to be said that very few of the defeated team appeared in Iraq's next World Cup qualifying match.

Under the threat of more of the same, the Iraqi team faced Pakistan. A similar defeat would see the players being left to languish in a rat-infested prison while a win would grant them the luxury of staying alive – until the next match, anyway. Fortunately, Iraq beat Pakistan 6-2 and everyone breathed a sigh of relief. Until their next defeat, a comprehensive 3-1 drubbing in Kazakhstan. Iraq were out of the World Cup.

In a country where missing persons could keep *Crimewatch* on the air 24 hours a day, seven days a week, the fate of the players remains unknown. It was feared that the team members were gunned down, cremated and scattered in the desert. After all, Uday's World Cup fury would have been further incited by Iraq's arch regional rivals, Iran, and their successful qualification.

To add fuel to the fire, Uday Hussein is no stranger to the law of the bullet. In 1996, he narrowly cheated death at the hands of a gunman who pumped ten bullets into him. In hospital after the attack, Uday married his fifteen-year-old cousin in a bizarre bid to prove his genitalia still worked despite his injuries. He spent six months recovering from the shooting.

Foreign diplomats are still making enquiries as to the whereabouts of the team but so far have only been able to confirm that Iraqi soccer boss, Zmetk Halai, was publicly flogged after a World Cup qualifying defeat by Cyprus for failing to include Saddam Hussein's nephew in the starting line-up.

Another team disappeared on 27 April 1993, although on the face of it the explanation is perfectly straightforward. Eighteen members of the Zambian World Cup squad died when their plane dived into the sea off Gabon. However, it is an incident shrouded in uncertainty as neither the families nor the supporters have been officially told why it happened.

The amount of travelling involved in the African World Cup qualifying group is huge, underlined by the vastness of the continent. On that fateful day, the Zambian squad were celebrating because they had beaten Mauritius 3-0 in an African Nations Cup tie the day before. The players had to spend a couple of hours on the tarmac at Libreville waiting for the next leg of their journey. The Zambian FA could not afford to hire a Zambian Airlines DC-8 so were forced to use a military plane designed for short-haul trips. The journey to their ultimate destination, Senegal, was 3,000 miles, and their first stop was the Congo capital Brazzaville – the halfway point. A two-hour flight would then take them on to Abidjan in the Ivory Coast when, after an overnight stop, they would make the last hop to Dakar to play Senegal in a vital World Cup qualifying tie.

The aircraft they were flying in was a DHC-5D Buffalo military aircraft bought in 1976 and refitted in 1991. Money in the Zambian FA was so tight that the players had slept in the plane the night before the Mauritius match as the FAZ (Football Association of Zambia) could not afford hotel rooms. According to reports, the Zambians were aware of some problems with the plane, but nothing too serious.

At 11 p.m. local time, the plane took off with its full load of 30 passengers. One of the ground crew noticed that on take-off, a wing was pointing slightly downward. An unusual manoeuvre he thought. Two minutes later, the plane exploded and crashed into the sea off the Gabonese coast, killing everyone on board.

Yet nobody knows what really happened as the crash became involved in the murky world of African international politics. There has been no official inquiry and the rumour mill is working overtime among Zambian fans. One theory is that the plane was shot down by a missile from a Gabon national guard military base, which, if true, could explain eye-witness accounts of an orange glowing light in the sky just before the plane crashed. Zambian reporters entertained this story – after all, the players were travelling on a hired military plane. The most persistent rumour, however, is that the team are still alive and being held captive in Gabon. This theory seems somewhat improbable due to the fact that 30 bodies were dragged from the sea by rescuers, although the theorists claim the bodies were Gabonese political prisoners.

When the flight left Brazzaville, an air controller is rumoured to have warned Libreville that the plane wasn't airworthy. The air controller allegedly made this claim to African soccer correspondent Jean-Gilbert Foutou, but the tape of the interview and the reporter's notes were confiscated by the Congolese government. Some witnesses insisted that the Libreville ground crew had implored the Zambians not to fly on the plane to Abidjan. Other eye-witness statements could not agree on whether the plane blew up in the air or when it landed. The fuselage still lies where the plane crashed – ten kilometres off the Gabonese coast in a mud bank. A further complication was the absence of a black box, which are not carried by military planes.

Rather than attempt to solve the mystery, both governments have simply traded insults. The Zambians accused the Gabonese of a cover up and Gabon hit back with the claim that the coffins sent by the Zambians for their dead players weren't up to international standards. The Zambians refused to issue an official report on the disaster, understandably leading to the frustrated widows of the players taking legal action.

The Zambians were nervous that any official crash report would put some of the blame on them, particularly over the

flight arrangements where costs were kept to a minimum –
it was fine to use a DC-8 to bring the players' bodies home
but not to travel on one to represent their country. The
situation was politically dangerous, compounded by the
emotional speech given by the Zambian president, Frederick
Chiluba, when the players were buried in what had become
sacred ground next to the national football stadium. Over
100,000 people watched the players being laid to rest.

However, the initial Zambian response to the crash was
commendable. A trust fund was set up for the bereaved
families and donations flooded in. The country was trawled
for new players and Freddie Mwila, a Zambian who had
played for the Atlanta Chiefs in the North American Soccer
League, was released from his contract as coach of Botswana
and given the job of rebuilding the national team.

Mwila built a new team with three old boys: the Bwayla
brothers, Kalusha and Joel, and Charles Musconda. They
hadn't been on flight AF319 because they played their club
football in Europe. On 4 July 1993, the new-look Zambia
took to the field at Lusaka's Independence Stadium against
Morocco. Morocco quickly went 1-0 up and the fans nearest
the cemetery stood up and turned towards the graves,
shouting, 'Where are you now that we need your help?'
Shortly afterwards, Kalusha Bwalya, who had led the team
out, scored from a direct free kick. The game ended Zambia
2, Morocco 1, and the fans claimed a miracle. In the return
leg in Casablanca, other group results meant the Zambians
had to win to qualify for the 1994 World Cup finals. They
lost 1-0.

It didn't help that the referee was Gabonese. Naturally,
fans back in Zambia were convinced that he favoured the
Moroccans. Resurgent rumours that the Gabonese military

had shot down flight AF319, coupled with this defeat, led 15,000 furious Zambians to flood on to the streets of the capital with banners declaring, 'The Gabonese have killed us twice.'

In 1994, however, the Zambians excelled themselves in the African Nations Cup and managed to reach the final where, despite taking an early lead, they lost 2-1 to Nigeria. But since then, Zambian football has slipped into turmoil, plagued by financial scandals, team walkouts over money and more bungling by the FAZ. Indeed, just two weeks before a World Cup qualifying tie in 1997 against South Africa, the entire squad went missing in a dispute over match allowances.

Today, the mystery surrounding Flight AF319 has not been solved. The widows of the eighteen fallen heroes are still waiting for a truthful account of the disaster and some haven't yet received money from the trust fund. Is it any wonder that so many Zambians turn to the graves of the dead team and pray? It is an African tradition that the spirits of the dead must be satisfied. The continual wrangling ensures that the eighteen players killed in April 1993 may have a long wait.

A universal attribute of players all over the world is the ability to brawl when the situation presents itself, and March 1997 saw perhaps the greatest ever football punch-up. Jamaica were in Mexico to play a couple of warm-up games before meeting the Mexican national side in a World Cup qualifying match. The Jamaicans played First Division side Toros Neza, quickly taking a 1-0 lead. Argentine-born Toros Neza player Arantxa lost his cool following a late tackle and all hell let loose. All 22 players, plus both benches, waded into a brawl, with several Jamaicans distinguishing themselves in combat. One such team member ran twenty yards to launch a high kick, studding the nape of an opponent's neck, while at least five other separate scuffles kicked off simultaneously.

After six minutes of fighting, there was a sudden stand-off. Both sides stood only feet apart, on the verge of restarting the conflict. Then all went quiet as the Jamaicans wandered off towards the touchline – to gather an arsenal of vicious weapons, including lumps of wood, stones, bricks, bottles and boots. Several Mexicans were badly hurt and ferried away from the stadium in ambulances. Understandably, the referee abandoned the match, leaving Jamaica's Brazilian coach, Rene Simoes, to try and explain his team's behaviour. 'The team simply lacks international experience,' he said.

For every media column inch that has praised Colombian Faustino Asprilla and his footballing skills, there has been another documenting his troubled life both on and off the pitch. Asprilla has a gift for finding trouble and in the past has been charged with possessing illegal weapons, firing guns into the air and kicking out a bus windscreen. In 1997, Colombian police claimed that the former Newcastle striker had sparked a fight during a rock concert in his home town. Colonel Jairo Salcedo, a top policeman in Tulua, south-west Colombia, alleged that Asprilla headbutted an officer at the concert in the local football stadium. 'Asprilla hit a policeman with his head while he was being removed from the place for verbally abusing members of the police,' he claimed.

In April of the same year, Asprilla clashed with Paraguay goalkeeper Jose Luis Chilavert while playing for Colombia in a World Cup qualifying game. Described at the time as 'the mother of all punch-ups', Chilavert hit Asprilla in the mouth (while the ball was in the centre circle), claiming that he had been provoked. Paraguay were leading 1-0 with less than fifteen minutes to go and it was almost suicide to give away a penalty at such an important stage in the game. Asprilla and Chilavert were sent off and, as Asprilla approached the bench, Chilavert spat at him. Colombian Victor Aristizabal decided to defend his team-mate and bulldozed into Chilavert, kicking off a brawl that included both benches.

The fight lasted a good ten minutes before it was broken up by police, who eventually allowed the game to restart. In the event, Colombia missed the penalty, Paraguay won 2-1 and both countries qualified for the World Cup finals in France. FIFA banned Chilavert for four games, Aristizabal for three and Tino Asprilla for two. Colombian manager Gustavo Moreno said, 'FIFA was too generous to Chilavert – he was to blame for everything.' Colombian midfielder Harold Lozano agreed, commenting, 'Chilavert should have been suspended for life. He's always causing trouble.'

The Paraguay captain is certainly no stranger to controversy. In 1996, he was given a three month suspended jail sentence for hitting a stadium assistant while playing for Velez Sarsfield and in late 1997 he was involved in a brawl with the aides of a top politician. The fight broke out when Chilavert was approached by men representing presidential candidate and former general Lino Oviedo in a hotel in Buenos Aires, who told him that Oviedo wanted to pay his respects to him. 'I told them no,' said Chilavert, 'because I think he put Paraguayan democracy in danger. Oviedo's aides started to insult me. Then they tried to attack me and I defended myself.'

In 1995, a South American Supercup match between

Brazilian sides Cruzeiro and Sao Paulo had to be called off after four Cruzeiro players were sent off and one went off injured. The match degenerated when Cruzeiro defender Rogeiro kicked an opponent and was sent off. Three Cruzeiro players protested too much and were also shown red cards. The match was abandoned early in the second half when Cruzeiro's Luis Fernando Gomes pulled up with a calf muscle injury. The team doctor said Gomes could not continue and as Cruzeiro had used all their substitutes, the referee had no option but to call the match off. Sao Paulo were leading 1-0.

Brazilian football is as inflammatory as it is skilful. In March 1997, the Flamengo coach, Paulo Autuori, offered to resign after his team were defeated by Vitoria 5-0 in the Brazilian Cup. He reluctantly agreed to stay on after discussions with the club's hierarchy but ran into more trouble a couple of weeks later. When Flamengo lost to Bangu, fans invaded the pitch and threw wooden sticks at the players. Back in Rio de Janeiro, Flamengo fans shot up the club's headquarters and one fan lobbed a grenade into the trophy room.

Dias Lima spent an hour locked in the dressing room after Botafogo's draw with Parana in Rio de Janeiro, a result which severely dented Botafogo's Championship chances. Lima was the match referee and on the final whistle found himself surrounded by furious Botafogo directors. When he eventually left the dressing room, he did so with a police escort, but was still showered with beer cans thrown by crazed fans, furious that he had ignored a succession of penalty appeals. Shaken and frightened, Lima was driven straight to the airport to make a swift getaway.

Brazilian fans don't just vent their spleen on match officials when things start to go wrong. Quite often, they turn on their own players. Pitarelli, goalkeeper for Guarani A side, who were flirting with relegation in 1996, needed urgent medical attention after being stoned by supporters while driving home from a match. Even more bizarrely, his colleague, Ailton, the club's No. 1 striker, was trapped in his own home for over a week when it was besieged by angry fans. Ailton was realistic about his predicament, telling reporters by phone, 'I don't like to go outside as I don't know what will happen to me.'

In 1997, a number of Brazilian teams battling against relegation used a number of underhand methods to avoid the drop from Serie 'A'. The Brazilian Football Federation, the CBF, received complaints alleging that some clubs were deliberately fielding ineligible players to try and win a few valuable points. Bahia argued that their opponents, Criciuma, played an ineligible player as a striker in a 3-0 win over them. Bragantino made a similar complaint after losing 3-0 to Vasco da Gama.

Fluminese, meanwhile, took footballing paranoia levels to new heights by beginning a campaign to prevent referees from any state that contained relegation-threatened clubs from refereeing their matches for fear of becoming victims of bribery. The CBF, aware that the number of sinners was significant, decided to consider pardoning the clubs involved, including the ones who were to be relegated. A precedent was set in 1996 when the two bottom clubs, Fluminese and Bragantino, were reinstated by the CBF just before the competition started. It was mooted that Serie 'A' – Brazilian football's top division – would be expanded to 32 clubs, thus lengthening the odds of relegation for the established clubs.

The CBF has bent over backward to ensure the big clubs have every chance of avoiding relegation. In 1995, they decreed that the bottom two teams would go down but that if one of those teams had previously won the Championship, they would get the chance to play off against the lowest placed non-Championship winners. A crazy system designed to halt corruption. Whatever happened to wholesome, healthy competition?

The infiltration of corruption in Brazilian football has been noticeable over the last few years but a big refereeing scandal came to light in the summer of 1997. The match that brought it to a head was a Brazilian Championship match between Vasco da Gama and Volta Redonda, which Vasco won 2-1. Vasco da Gama scored both their goals in the fourth and sixth minutes of injury time when Volta Redonda were already reduced to nine men. The 'unusual circumstances' of the match left the Vasco da Gama fans chanting 'It's a fix!' and 'Robbery!' even though their team had won. Match reports claimed that the referee, Duque, had 'invented and inverted fouls' and said the sendings off – which happened immediately after Volta took the lead – were extremely harsh. Volta Redondo stated to the CBF that they were victims of a complicated plot to get Americano, the club supported by Rio de Janeiro federation president Eduardo Viana, into the third stage of the Rio de Janeiro Championship. Football observers were united in their opinion of Mr Duque. 'His strategy is well known,' said one. 'He intimidates players, invents fouls so that they complain and can be given the yellow card, then he sends them off for a further offence.'

Sadly, rumours do not provide hard evidence, however clear cut it may seem to some, and Eduardo Viana did have one ally – Vasco da Gama vice-president Eurico Miranda. When asked about his club's bizarre victory and the chanting of the winning team's fans, he said, 'They were Flamengo fans disguised as Vasco da Gama fans.' The CBF conveniently chose to believe Miranda and swept the incident neatly under the carpet.

Out of all the domestic and international rivalries in South American football, none is more intense or frightening than that between Argentine clubs Boca Juniors and River Plate. Every game at Boca verges on legalised lunacy. The fans are as passionate as they come but are also fond of intimidation and violence as a way to get the required result. Boca Juniors play at the Bombonera Stadium and the home fans save their nastiest tricks specially for the visit of River Plate. Armed riot police line the streets on the approach to the stadium to prevent the Boca Ultras (the Bara Brava) and their River Plate counterparts causing mayhem. Inside the ground, the football takes a back seat as 60,000 fans chant abuse and let off flares that could quite easily kill or maim.

The background to the ill feeling between the supporters is a political one with the usual complications. Boca are the working-class team while River Plate, who used to play in the Boca area, are now located in a more middle-class part of Buenos Aires. The history of trouble between the clubs is long and regular. In 1994, twelve Boca Bara Brava were jailed for murdering three River Plate fans in a drive-by shooting. One of them has since died in prison from an Aids-related illness but fans' banners around the ground still commemorate them as 'heroes' of the Boca cause.

The spectre of drugs is feared within world football and none more so than in Colombia, where the drugs cartels buy clubs specifically to launder money made from their illegal activities (see *Football Babylon*). The Colombian authorities have battled hard against the problem but it has proved extremely difficult to tackle successfully. In August 1997, a Colombian police report revealed that the domestic game was still being financed by the drugs cartels on a massive scale, stating that out of 142 main shareholders in the country's sixteen First Division clubs, 80 are wanted on drugs charges. The police and the anti-corruption authorities face an ongoing game of cat and mouse with the cartels' overlords, many paying the ultimate price for their investigations.

Out of all the players who have used narcotics, Diego Maradona is undoubtedly the most high profile. Already banned twice from football for drug abuse, he faced a third ban after failing a dope test on 24 August 1997. This test was carried out after he played for Boca Juniors against his first professional club, Argentinos Juniors, a match which ended 4-2 to Boca.

Maradona was first banned in 1991 after helping Napoli to beat Bari 10-0 and at the 1994 World Cup finals he tested positive for 'a cocktail of stimulants' after Argentina's win over Greece. In 1997, Maradona's manager at Boca Juniors was Fuillermo Coppola, himself jailed on cocaine charges in 1996, and he gave reporters his reaction to the latest charges against his star player. 'It can't be. There must have been a mistake.' Coppola then went on to claim that someone had spiked Maradona's drink. A second test was ordered and on 4 September another positive result was recorded. Maradona's lawyers were not happy and ordered that a DNA check be carried out to confirm that the urine used for the tests did in fact belong to their client.

'I will always test positive for drugs, because I will always speak up about my enemies,' said Maradona. 'If I had taken cocaine I wouldn't have gone to the match. Cocaine doesn't help but rather hinders you on the pitch – I know I would see four balls and eight defenders.'

The positive test stood. Maradona was suspended but continued to train with Boca Juniors. On 12 September he earned the right to carry on playing pending a disciplinary inquiry but five days later was hit by the news that the Argentinian court of appeal had turned down his appeal challenging a four-year prison sentence. The jail term was handed out by a provincial court following an incident in Buenos Aires when Maradona allegedly injured four reporters using an air rifle. The case has not yet been finalised, with Maradona's lawyers seeking to trade a prison sentence for an extensive period of community service. Legal experts in Argentina do not rate Maradona's chances very highly.

In 1997, Maradona, a tortured and broken man, spoke of retiring to a life in Cuba as he is friendly with the country's dictator, Fidel Castro. 'I'd go for Fidel, the climate and because I get on very well with Cubans,' he said.

On 30 October 1997, his 37th birthday, Maradona retired from football for the sixth time. The last straw for him, he said, was the rumour that he had tested positive after his last match for Boca Juniors against River Plate. But it may have been his performance in that match that finally convinced him to hang up his boots. He was no longer up to top-level football and was substituted at half time. Maradona has out-retired David Bowie but unlike the singer, it is almost certain that he will never play professionally again.

Years ago, Australia was a footballing outpost, but today its emergence as a serious football nation is almost complete – with no small thanks to a certain T. Venables Esq. Australian football concentrates on ethnic grouping rather than totally mixed-race sides, although this has begun to change over the last few years. Anyone who has watched or follows Australian rugby would never question the strength of the players, an attitude that has certainly not been lost on some of Australia's football fans. One Adelaide City player, Costanzo, was left blinded in one eye after rival fans attacked his team's bus with bottles and rocks. Clearly displeased with their team's 2-0 defeat, a gang of up to twenty youths were involved as the bus left South Melbourne's home ground. Two other players, Dino Mennillo and John Gibson, also suffered cuts at the hands of the fans. During the game itself, in which two players were shown red cards, an assistant referee was also injured when bottles were thrown at him.

Costanzo underwent emergency treatment at the Royal Melbourne Hospital, where surgeons removed slivers of glass from his eye. 'It was very scary,' said Adelaide City captain Alex Tobin. 'When a mob takes control, dangerous things can happen – and they did. All the players basically got down on the floor of the bus to shelter from the broken glass, bricks and bottles that were being thrown into the vehicle.'

Paraguay supporters are slightly more gentlemanly in their choice of missiles. During a match between home side Sportivo Luqueno and Vitoria of Brazil, fans pelted players with fruit. However, the referee chose to abandon the match when the initial shower of oranges suddenly got heavier on account of the bricks, coins and bottles that rained down from the stands. The Sportivo fans were upset that their side were trailing 4-1.

When Egypt played Morocco in 1997, Egyptian star Ibrahim Hassan received a life ban from football for making 'obscene gestures' at the Morocco fans. Hassan tried to explain his actions: 'It was like a war. Everywhere we went in Morocco, people verbally abused us and spat at us.' Hassan claimed that Moroccan hooligans set fire to Egypt's flag and lobbed metal ball bearings at their players. 'The gesture was an action taken in difficult circumstances,' he said.

Even animals have been used by rival fans. In the Seville region of Spain, Real Betis supporters paint green stripes on to white rabbits (Betis' colours) and send them racing across the pitch. One such painted rabbit managed to evade the tackles of three Real Madrid players in a meeting between the two clubs, before surrendering and allowing itself to be caught by a Betis steward.

The Australian game is compartmentalised into largely ethnic teams, depending on which country has immigrants in certain areas. In Melbourne one interesting match is played between two predominantly Maltese teams – Sunshine George Cross and Green Gully Ajax. Whenever they play each other, George Cross supporters taunt their cowardly rivals with cries of 'Chicken!' and throw live poultry sprayed green on to the pitch. They also encourage the chickens to distract Ajax's goalkeeper.

It is almost unheard of for a side to make a public apology for their bad form, yet that is exactly what the Chinese national squad did after they failed to reach the 1998 World Cup finals in France. The Chinese were simply dreadful in the qualifying games and the players apologised to the nation in an open letter: 'We let you down again. We are overwhelmed by remorse and self-scolding. We want to say a sincere sorry to everyone. We know little about the rapidly developing world of football and the Chinese team needs improvements in management, training and quality of players. We will thoroughly review our qualifying competition and sum up the lessons.'

Refreshing honesty from a country that has potentially far more footballers than all the other countries in the world put together.

Even Russian president Boris Yeltsin has noted the value to national morale of a successful team. Yeltsin announced in early 1998 that he may take personal control of the Russian team after they bombed out of the World Cup. 'The president was displeased with the poor performance of Russia's players who failed to show true Russian character,' said his spokesman. Football watchers put Yeltsin's outburst down to too much vodka but, with Boris, you are never quite sure what he will do next.

7 Fans

I T'S AN OLD CLICHÉ – but without fans football would not exist. supporters are the lifeblood of a club. They celebrate the highs and suffer the lows and, despite their commitment, are asked to pay ever-spiralling costs in pursuit of their passion. Critics say that fans who complain about their lot should terminate their love affair with football and do something else instead. Economically sound, without a doubt, but the people who make those sorts of suggestions have neither experienced nor understand what it's like to support a football team. As someone once said, 'You can change your car or even your wife, but you can never change your football club.' Emotionally, being a supporter is one of the most mentally unsound things you can do. It affects your moods, your relationships and even your health. Let's face it, you've got to be mad to travel 200 miles on a wet Wednesday in January for a 33 and a third chance of happiness. Unlike players and board members, who invariably travel to a game in relative luxury, the fans have to be hardy and resilient.

It is for these reasons that supporters resent arrogant board members who abuse their positions through actions that make the fans feel unimportant. It will be a great day for football when *all* club chairmen accept and recognise that they are merely custodians of a club, which will still be there long after they are dead and buried.

Players have a responsibility, too, not only to themselves but to their employers – the fans. In an ideal world, the players wouldn't get paid at all if they lost a game. Of course, football is not a perfect game played in a perfect world but perhaps clubs should try and compensate supporters for bad performances. A credit/debit bank account system would work, providing the supporters agreed. Imagine a system where a season ticket for a club cost, say, £350. If the team won, the club could rest assured that they were giving supporters value for money and add £5 on to the cost of next year's season ticket account, and so on for each victory. If a team lost, they would reduce the cost of next year's account by £5 for each defeat, with no change for a draw. To make the system slightly more arbitrary, an independent set of adjudicators could assess a side out of ten. A score below six would mean a debit to the account and vice versa for a victory. This would at least make the club and the players more accountable to the fans, and surely the vast majority would be prepared to pay more for the privilege of watching if they had had value for money the previous season.

Win, lose or draw, some fans go to extraordinary lengths to watch their team play. Among the most impressive are a small but elite bunch who travel from foreign lands to watch their heroes. Devoted Newcastle fan Graham Edmondson is a fine example. Even though he emigrated to Dallas, Texas, several years ago, he still flies back to the north-east once a month to watch his beloved Newcastle United play at St James's Park. Each flight alone costs him over £300.

Barnsley fanatic Alison Saxby, 31, travels from her home

in France at Bapaume on the Somme for every home game at Oakwell. She works as a gardener for the First World War War Graves Commission and has to leave home at 1.30 a.m. on the Saturday morning of a home game to catch an early-morning ferry which arrives in Dover at 6 a.m. Then she catches a train to London, arriving at 9 a.m. The Express service to Doncaster leaves London, King's Cross, at 10.30 a.m. and when Alison reaches her destination she is met by her father, Alan, who drives her to Barnsley for the game. Her devotion to the Tykes costs about £100 per trip, including fares and the price of her season ticket. Alison, who was born in Barnsley, says, 'When I get back to France I am shattered. People think I'm mad but it's money well spent. The atmosphere is electric. They play lovely football. I hate it when they lose but it's wonderful to see them.' Barnsley Football Club describe Alison as 'a true supporter'.

Travelling from Europe to the UK for a match may seem suspect to many but to travel from Australia is surely almost certifiable. One such trip went horribly wrong.

Wolves fan Christos Konospiris saved up £800 for a flight to England from his native Australia to watch Wanderers in action at Molineux on the last day of the 1995/96 season. In high spirits, he turned up at Molineux only to find that Wolves were playing away at Charlton, 130 miles away.

Another Antipodean trip to England did not go exactly to plan for Chelsea fan Gary Adams in April 1997. Adams lives in Sydney and planned to travel to London with his girlfriend, Helen, for the first time in six years. He remembers his trip with uncomfortable ease. 'As soon as I knew the dates for the trip I rang my mate in London and asked him to get some tickets for Chelsea. I was thrilled when he told me that he had managed to get some for the game against Arsenal. All the way over on the plane I was thinking about getting back to the Bridge and seeing the Blues in action again. And not against some dull side like Wimbledon or Bolton, but in a top London derby.

'The first disappointment was when the Chelsea team was announced. No Wise, Di Matteo, LeBoeuf, Hughes, Gullit or Duberry – all injured or suspended. Instead we had a couple of stars like Vialli and Zola playing alongside a bunch of kids and a few old crocks like Erland Johnsen and Paul Parker. Arsenal were at full strength so we weren't too confident. It was great to be back at the ground but the team were awful and got completely stuffed. It was a bit hard to take, having travelled all that way, especially when I'd seen us play so well in televised matches.'

As Adams left the ground after the match, events took an unusual turn. 'When we were leaving the ground, for some reason a piece of paper on the ground caught my eye. It turned out to be a betting slip for that afternoon's Grand National [the match kicked off in the morning as it was on live television]. There were two bets on it for a total of £40 which would win about £500 if they came off. It seemed like a good omen so we went to a pub to watch the race. We thought the race was a long time in starting and eventually I asked somebody what had happened as we had lost track of time over a few beers. I was told that the race had been cancelled because of a bomb threat. My girlfriend said that I should take the betting slip back to the bookies and claim the stake money. "It would be like finding forty quid in the street," she said, and would cover the cost of the Chelsea tickets. But I decided to hang on to it when it was announced that the race would be rerun. Of course, that was the wrong decision as neither of the horses even managed to finish the race.'

A hundred South African fans had a far more harrowing experience when they travelled to London for the 1996 Cup Final between Manchester United and Liverpool at Wembley. The fans had paid £4,000 each for the round trip, which included a ticket to the final. For many of them, it was the trip of a lifetime. On Cup Final day, they all boarded their luxury coach and were transported to the famous twin towers, only to be turned away at the turnstile. Their tickets were from a batch that had gone missing from the Liverpool allocation and consequently had been reported stolen/ missing and were no longer valid. One of the party, lawyer Ivor Lazerson, said, 'The hurtful thing is that they were completely without sympathy. They just said, "Get out of the way. You're blocking the aisle." ' The party managed to watch the final on television, something they could have done back home in South Africa.

Dedication separates the supporting men from the boys, some so obsessed by their clubs that they will go to extraordinary lengths to follow them. Dave Burnley, a Burnley supporter, hasn't missed a Clarets match since 10 April 1974. Burnley were playing Newcastle United away and because the match was rearranged at 24 hours' notice, he was unable to go. He vowed that he wouldn't miss another game and so far he hasn't.

Similarly, Mick Derby has only missed one domestic Derby County match, an evening game at Newport, in his two decades or more as a Rams fan. Not that he didn't try to get there. 'I got as far as Gloucester and realised that the train would get me there after the final whistle.' He also missed an away game in the Anglo-Italian Cup. 'Coming back from the previous match in Italy, we'd been delayed. I was already on a final warning at work and I was sacked.

The rest of the lads were magnificent and got me reinstated pending a disciplinary hearing. Unfortunately, it happened to clash with out next Italian game. After much soul searching, I felt honour bound to attend the hearing,' says Derby.

As you may have guessed, both Dave and Mick changed their names by deed poll to demonstrate their depth of feelings for their clubs. Dave changed his surname to Burnley in 1976. 'It was our last season in the top flight,' said Dave. 'It made the local and national papers. Of course, I get some stick for it, but I have never been ashamed to confront it. I will support Burnley for as long as possible. It's my destiny,' adds Dave.

Mick Derby did a lot of deliberating before he took the plunge when he was just twenty. 'I thought long and hard about it before deciding it was what I really wanted to do. I got a lot of flak from my mother. Then the evening paper and the match programme picked up on it. Soon everyone knew about me, my name and the fact that I try to go to every reserve and youth game. Even today, if I'm having a drink in town, people come up to me and say, "What are you doing here? I heard the Under 14s have a friendly at St Ives," but it's all good natured. I once waited outside the ground for an hour for Jim Smith to come out because I'd heard a rumour about a pre-season game at Lincoln City. He was very helpful, shook my hand and wished me all the best,' remembers Mick fondly.

Thirty-eight-year-old Caledonian Thistle fan Ker Campbell has seen every match played by the team since the club was formed following the merger of Inverness Thistle and Inverness Caledonian in 1995. Campbell is on the dole but still manages to make the 90-mile round trip for every home League game, as well as all the away games. He's also the only fan to have seen every single senior match – a record he set on a pre-season warm-up game in Stonaway in the Outer Hebrides. Rather sadly but perhaps not surprisingly, Campbell was the only Caledonian Thistle supporter there.

Of course, some footballing obsessions can end in tears. Brian, a postman, is an Arsenal season ticket holder and his passion for his club lost him his wife. 'When I first got married I was working nights at the Post Office in London. I'd been married about a week and a half. I went down to the pub for a few drinks in the early hours at Smithfield Market and they'd all go, "Are you coming to watch Newcastle versus Arsenal?" About six pints later, there I am halfway up the M1. I'd gone, hadn't I? I got back on Monday after leaving on Saturday morning and the old cases were outside the house. That was the start of the end I think,' said Brian.

Perfect days – three points, trouble-free travel and a trip executed with clockwork precision – are fantastic when they happen but inevitably it's the disastrous trips that enter football folklore. In the 1982/83 season, Spurs played in Europe and were drawn against Bayern Munich. It was a 1-1 draw at White Hart Lane and the second leg was to take place in Bavaria a couple of weeks later. Tottenham fan Paul Woozley travelled to Munich, a city he was familiar with as he had spent a couple of months living there in 1982. 'The previous summer I had spent three splendid months in Munich where my father was working. So when the draw paired us with Bayern I had to make the trip. Hours trundled past on the coach. Singing, drinking, stretching cramped legs, but not sleeping. This was torture beyond my imagination. I lost all track of time, but it must have taken eighteen hours,' said Paul.

'On arrival, the police wouldn't let us go anywhere for five hours before escorting us to the stadium. And here is the crux of the story. After the journey from hell came the game from hell. It felt like minus 50 degrees on the terrace and then the fog came down. The match went ahead but I couldn't see any of it. The occasional roar could have been a goal for Bayern – who knows? We couldn't see the scoreboard. All I know is that the fog cleared for me to see Houghton score for Spurs. An equaliser? A consolation? Or did it put us ahead? Apparently, we lost 4-1 and so it was back to the coach for the horrific journey to London. In summary, I sacrificed three days and lots of money to stand on a terrace in Bavaria watching fog.'

Sometimes events can conspire against you but actually work in your favour, as Swansea fanatic Mark Evans discovered on Boxing Day in 1987. Swansea were playing at Crewe and Evans had arranged to travel there with some friends in a hired coach. Evans takes up the story. 'I'd gone to the local for Christmas night to have a few beers with the lads. The coach to Crewe left at 8.30 the next morning, and I said to my mates, "Tell me when you're going home or I'll miss the bus." But I carried on drinking until 3.30 a.m. And the next thing I knew I woke up in a chair in the pub. I asked the cleaner the time. 9.30 a.m! There were no trains. I phoned my mate but he was staying in bed. So I phoned a taxi firm and said, "I'm desperate." They picked me up, I fell asleep in the back and when I woke up we were in Crewe. But by 2 p.m. there was no sign of the other Swansea fans – they'd broken down in Birmingham and never made it! Was it fate that I missed the coach? It cost me £100 but it was worth it.'

One intensely unlucky England fan had a disappointing

evening when he tried to go to the England–Holland friendly at Wembley in March 1988. Michael Ireson was keen to check out England's form ahead of the 1988 European Championships in Germany and he was almost meticulous in his preparation. 'I left work at four o'clock, knowing it would take an hour and a half to get to Wembley. The traffic was heavier than usual and I arrived at six o'clock. A kind car park attendant relieved me of £4 for the privilege of squeezing my car into a tight space. The only problem was that I didn't have a ticket. I stopped a steward who informed me that the game was a sell-out. It was now 7 p.m. and I resigned myself to watching the highlights on *Sportsnight*. Trudging back to my car, feeling most sorry for myself, I was stopped in my tracks as my worst nightmare came into sight. My motor was blocked in on all sides!

'I got into my car, switched on the radio and spent the evening listening to a game going on 200 yards behind me. I eventually got out of the car park at 10.30 p.m. and arrived home at midnight, too late to catch the action with Des Lynam,' lamented Ireson.

Scotland fan Roger Cooper will never forget a trip to Berne for a World Cup qualifier before the 1994 tournament. 'I travelled alone but met up with a couple of Scots on the Seacat. This proved to be my downfall because one of them, Geordie, had two bottles of vodka. By the time we reached Berne, we were very much the worse for drink, but that didn't stop us buying more. Come four o'clock, a few hundred pissed and merry jocks had gathered in the main square around a fountain.'

Things started to go steadily downhill. 'What possessed me to do it, I don't know, but I climbed up the concrete sprinkler to tie my scarf round the sphere at the top,

although I'm shit-scared of heights. All I remember is falling
– the rest was recounted to me later. My arm hit the side of
the fountain with such a force that the elbow joint almost
snapped in two. I needed eighteen stitches in a head wound,
too. I swallowed my tongue and stopped breathing as well.
Thankfully, a Dundee fan who was playing the pipes had
met up with an Irish nurse and she saved my life. I was taken
to hospital, sprayed sick on the floor and was told I needed
surgery on my arm. But I wanted to see the game so I
discharged myself in time for the second half with the score
at 1-1. The final score was 3-1 to the Swiss. I spent the rest
of the night in hospital due to a relapse.

'The journey home on the train wasn't much better. I was in
a cabin with someone who couldn't speak a word of anything.
My arm was in plaster, hanging over the edge of the bunk, and
I was in a lot of pain and sporting a dreadful hangover. The
only consolation was that England didn't qualify either.'

Let's not forget, however, that away trips can be surreal
for the players as well as the fans. Arsenal and England's
Alan Smith remembers all too well a truly weird overseas
trip to play an International. It was 1989 and England were
playing Albania in a World Cup qualifier. Despite being told
that the country was a little behind the times, the players
didn't realise quite how much until they had collected their
luggage and left the airport building. Smith takes up the
story: 'The locals were all wearing old brown and grey suits
with flared trousers, wide lapel jackets and kipper ties. They
couldn't stop staring at us as we sat on the coach waiting to
leave for our hotel. In our fashionable England tracksuits
[Are you sure, Alan?] we must have looked like beings from
another planet. The journey to the capital, Tirana, was
delayed by farmers on horse and carts and sheep wandering

along a main road that at times was little more than a dirt track. The hotel was the best one in Albania but the beds sank into a 'U' shape when you lay on them and the only form of entertainment was seeing who could kill the most cockroaches in the bathrooms.'

The Albanians were football fanatics and England allowed quite a crowd to watch one of their training sessions. In typical Gazza style, Paul Gascoigne took it upon himself to give the spectators a bit of a show by going in goal. He had no trouble winning them over and rapturous applause greeted his every save.

Some years later, Smith travelled with England's 'B' team to Russia to play the CIS. Having played their game, the squad went to watch the full International the following day in Moscow. It turned out to be a hair-raising occasion for Smith. 'After the match we waited on the coach outside the ground for the first team to get changed. It was taking some time so to relieve the boredom a couple of our lads had the bright idea of putting a big wad of roubles through the sunroof on to the top of the coach. Inflation being what it is in Russia, the notes weren't actually worth that much but the Russian fans in the car park weren't going to know that. When the coach drove off, the money flew into the air as planned and dropped to the ground like ticker-tape. A mad scrabble ensued behind us.

'Our coach was stopped and a high-ranking offical stormed on to the bus. He made me stand up for no reason that I could see, other than that I was the first person he clapped eyes on. There was plenty of finger pointing as he ranted away in Russian, and I had visions of being carted away to the Kremlin for questioning. Everyone looked at me in silence. I felt my face redden, while at the back of the coach there were muffled sniggers from the real culprits.'

In September 1997, 700 Leicester City fans travelled to Madrid for a UEFA Cup tie against Atletico Madrid. Little did they know that the trip would turn into a living nightmare. The coach journey took 33 hours and the Foxes fans were only given two opportunities to stop for refreshments along the way. When they arrived in the Spanish capital, they were corralled into penned areas by a less-than-welcoming gun-toting police force – UEFA had deemed that the match was a high-risk category necessitating a large police presence. Sightseeing was out of the question and after the match the Leicester fans were kept behind in the stadium until well after midnight, before being herded back to their convoy of fourteen coaches.

The appalling treatment prompted a deluge of complaints. Fans contacted solicitors, who took statements of kidney disorders and stomach complaints. Tony Roe, who filmed the trip for BBC Midlands, said, 'It was those fans who could least afford to go to Europe who took the cheapest way there and they are the ones who are now wondering if they want to go again. The whole thing was horrific.'

Gary Silke, Leicester fanzine editor, who flew out for the game, added, 'For many of them it should have been the proudest moment of their football-supporting lives and yet some were in tears.'

Leicester offered the fans compensation in the form of a £35 voucher which could only be spent in Leicester's two club shops. Having paid £115 for the coach trip, this wasn't received gratefully and the City Council's Consumer Protection Service branded the hand-out as stingy and completely inadequate. Responding to this criticism, Leicester chairman Tom Smeaton, an Australian businessman, issued a statement saying: 'We cannot be held solely responsible for what happened. We launched our immediate investigation into what went wrong, and I am sure that many valuable lessons have been learned. We have also given various undertakings to Leicester City Council concerning future away trips, because we are determined that things should never go so badly wrong again.'

The £35 compensation vouchers were not even enough to buy a replica shirt, at the time retailing at £39.99. Councillor Ted Cassidy, chairman of the council's Environment and Development Committee, urged the club to increase the pay-out. 'Leicester supporters feel that £35 is a derisory figure compared with the enormous discomfort they endured, and it would be difficult not to sympathise with them,' he said.

Perhaps one way to ensure that your fans travel in style is to do what Lincoln City did in November 1997. Cash-strapped City came up with a highly unusual way of raising funds by letting paying fans on to the team coach to travel to away matches. The club charged £30 per person (including a match ticket) for short away trips and £80 per person for matches further afield (including an overnight hotel stay, dinner, lunch and match ticket). It was also a chance for Lincoln fans to witness first hand the unconventional management style of John Beck, who after one defeat threw cold water over his players. 'It was John's idea, and if he wasn't happy with it all, we wouldn't have done it,' explained Gerry Lonsdale, Lincoln's marketing director. 'All the fans have to sign a good behaviour agreement, but then they're hardly known for causing trouble anyway.'

Ron Myland was one of the first supporters to take advantage of the scheme, travelling with the players to their match against Notts County. 'The players were all friendly and chatted away,' he said. 'John Beck even came over and started talking to us. He was telling us how he was going to play the match, what his team was and what tactics he was going to use.' All very cosy, but what if an opposing team's supporter bought a ticket on the Lincoln coach?

The decision to introduce the scheme was a purely financial one and was piloted when Lincoln played Exeter away on the last day of the 1996/97 season. John Beck decided to fill the eight empty seats on the team coach for away trips because he knew that as a lower-league club, Lincoln needed to grasp every money-generating activity. Although it impinges on the players' privacy, the revenue the scheme generates allows a few extra overnight stops before matches, helping the side to be better prepared for matches. As a result, Lincoln are in a healthy financial state, and according to Gerry Lonsdale it increases the club's influence in the Lincoln area. 'We still have to do everything we can to make money. We are also anxious to open up every aspect of the club to the community. Inviting supporters to travel with the players to away trips is all part of that.'

Coach drivers are the unsung heroes of any football club's away trips but sometimes plans can go awry. Stoke fan Ian Fenton will never forget a tortuous trip to Oldham on the opening day of the 1996/97 season. 'Anyone who has ever travelled to Boundary Park will know how easy it is – M6 on to the M62 then the A627 (M) and the ground, one of the highest above sea level, is clear to spot as you come off the slip road. Instead, our driver came off the M62 at an earlier junction and headed north. It was when we passed Bolton's Bunden Park (their old stadium) that we realised we were heading in the wrong direction. Next, we noticed a throng in blue and white shirts supping outside pubs and there was Ewood Park, ready for the Blackburn v. Tottenham game. The time was now 2.35 p.m. and even the shyest passengers were beginning to vent their anger. We were near Accrington when we saw a sign for Manchester. Even then the driver ignored it. He only turned round when a chorus of angry voices pointed out his latest error. He got on the right road at last and Boundary Park was visible. We got into the ground at 2.56 p.m. The nightmare continued when Stoke keeper Mark Prudhoe went off injured in the first half. The reserve keeper, Carl Muggleton, had got stuck in traffic jams on the motorway and arrived at the ground at 2.45, too late for the 2.30 deadline to be included in the team. So defender Ian Cranston went between the posts. Thankfully, Stoke went on to win 2-1. There was no collection for the driver on the way home!'

Early in 1997, a group of Fulham fans were on a coach, under the impression that they were on their way to see their team play at Colchester. Only they were travelling in the wrong direction and following signs to Cambridge instead. The fans vociferously tried to persuade the driver to turn round but he refused, taking them all the way to Cambridge. They missed the match, which Fulham lost 2-1. Oh, well, for every cloud there is a silver lining.

Sometimes, and perhaps more crucially, transportation doesn't even turn up for the players. In May 1997, Aston Villa travelled to California for an end-of-season tour/ holiday. Four UK-based Villa fans and two exiled Brummies went to San Francisco airport to meet the late arrivals – new signing Stan Collymore and Villa manager Brian Little. The fans were chatting to Collymore as he signed autographs when Litle approached, looking worried because there was no sign of their American greeting party. The Villa fans stepped in and offered to drive the Villa duo to the team base, a Hyatt hotel in the city centre. To thank them, Little took it upon himself to change the team's plans and agreed to spend the afternoon in the Mad Dog in the Fog bar which was owned by one of the exiled fans. It was a historic occasion for Villa because it was the first time new signing Stan Collymore had met up with his new team-mates. One of the Villa fans, Dave Woodhall, said, 'We tried to get Doug Ellis to buy a round – though we'd have more chance trying to get him to sign Ronaldo!'

On the subject of alcohol, a Southampton University student was adamant that he did not want to go to a nightclub offering pints of beer at 10p a pint because he was far more interested in spending his evening at Selhurst Park watching Crystal Palace play Reading. It turned out to be the wrong decision, as Andrew Worden remembers: 'Despite the persistent drizzle outside, we jumped on the first train to south London. In my haste, I forgot my Young Person's Railcard, meaning I had to fork out £19 [which would have bought him 190 pints of lager . . .].

'As we got off the train, we saw a distinct lack of replica Palace shirts in the area. But cheered by the weather, which seemed to have cleared, we carried on. Five minutes later we arrived at Selhurst Park but to our amazement the floodlights were unlit and the gate unopened. Something was wrong. A helpful steward told us that the match had been cancelled an hour beforehand because of a waterlogged pitch. Between expletives, we desperately tried to remember where else in London there was a match – Barnet v. Lincoln was the only one we could recall and that was on the other side of London. Dispirited after an hour's pointless wandering around, we got back on the train thinking things couldn't get any worse. At that point a bright light appeared in the distance and the train cruised past the New Den, where Millwall and Notts County were playing on a perfect pitch in front of an enthusiastic crowd.'

Even sadder, perhaps, is the story of Grimsby fan Mike Rowell, who cycled 180 miles to London to see the Mariners play West Ham in the fourth round of the FA Cup in January 1996. When Rowell reached the front of Upton Park, he found that the gates were locked, the game having been postponed due to a frozen pitch. If only he had remembered to take his portable radio with him.

Away fans are always in the minority but lifelong Wigan fan, Steve McKevitt, gave the situation a whole new meaning in the 1994/95 season. Having travelled to Mansfield, he had to endure 25 minutes of personal abuse from the home fans when it transpired that he was the only away supporter to have made the trip south for the Third Division fixture.

'I don't often get to home games because I live in Sheffield, but Mansfield is only down the road so I decided to go,' he remembers. 'I was meeting some friends there, but when I turned up they weren't where I was supposed to meet them. I thought they must have gone in already. But when I got inside there weren't any Wigan fans in – I was the first poor sod to arrive. It wouldn't have been so bad, but loads of Mansfield fans were already in at the home end. I sat on the terrace reading my programme, but all the time the Mansfield fans were chanting louder and louder. I was trying to work out what they were singing – the match hadn't even started – and then I realised they were singing at me.

'It was like a nightmare. I got the full works: "Where's your skateboard parked?" "What's it like to have no mates?" "We know who you are, you are gonna die" . . . it went on for ages. It was getting really embarrassing, so I went to the toilet, but even then I could hear them singing, "Where's the queer gone?" I bought a pie on the way back, but it just gave them something else to sing. "You fat bastard", "Who ate all the pies?" This went on for 25 minutes until finally the Wigan fans turned up. I remember thinking, Thank God!'

At least McKevitt got to the match on time, which is more than can be said for two Blackburn Rovers fans who travelled to Warsaw for a Champions' League game. Rovers played Legia Warsaw in October 1995 and the two fans chose to pop into a brothel for a bit of pre-match entertainment. They were told by the hostess that they were welcome to watch the match on television but as enticing as the Polish beauties were, they paled into insignificance when compared with Rovers live in the flesh. Arriving late at the ground, they witnessed one solitary Legia goal that condemned Blackburn Rovers to their third consecutive defeat in the Champions' League. Colin Alred, another Blackburn fan on the same trip, said, 'It was a real experience. I'm glad I did it. Just one complaint – the coach driver only seemed to have one tape, a sixties compilation. I never want to hear a Roy Orbison song ever again.'

One experience that Bristol City fan Tracey Peters will never forget is her trip to Portsmouth a couple of years ago. Twenty-stone Tracey had an argument with a turnstile. 'It was my first trip to Pompey's ground,' said Tracey. 'The turnstiles are narrow and made of really hard rubber. There isn't room for an inch of surplus lard, and mine measured in feet rather than inches. I moved in between the stiles, slowly squidging my hips and thighs into the rubber prison, thinking I might actually get through them, when all of a sudden I couldn't move. "I'm stuck!" I whispered to my sister, who was behind me. "No, you're not, you daft cow," she hissed. "Just get a move on." The more I wiggled my hips, the more they flooded into the gaps in the bars like jelly in a mould. My sister tried to push me through the stiles. The people behind my sister started pushing as well, and just when I really thought I'd be stuck until they called the fire brigade, I shot out like a cork from a bottle. I was dripping with sweat and bright red with embarrassment. I grabbed my sister, threw some money at the blokes on the gate, who were laughing their heads off, and we ran into the stands to hide.

'Worse was to come. I noticed people staring at me and giggling. You're just imagining it, I thought to myself, until I heard the unmistakable strains of "Who ate all the pies?" floating across the terraces. It was the worst moment of my life – the whole crowd joined in and they were all singing and pointing at me. All I wanted was for a hole to open up in the ground – although I probably couldn't have got through that, either.'

Tracey's turnstile problems will never be repeated. She has shed eight stones since her Fratton Park nightmare.

Long-distance travel is a necessity of football and players and fans spend hours shuttling up and down the country's motorway system from fixture to fixture. For the lucky few, there are more luxurious methods for getting from A to B but for most supporters, travelling is a long, arduous business fraught with pitfalls.

Eric Pickup, 52-year-old chairman of the Scarborough Supporters and Social Club, editor of the club programme and organiser of away travel, is a typical die-hard fan. 'It's ingrained in me,' he says. 'I couldn't imagine not following the Boro.' Eric does admit to getting a bit down sometimes, particularly when things don't go according to plan. 'I travelled all the way to Torquay. It took hours, we got there and they called off the match. That could have been depressing, but me and my wife stayed over, made a weekend of it.'

QPR fan Michael Telfer remembers a particular bale of hay which almost caused him to miss a match at Old Trafford. 'We were about an hour from Manchester when what looked like a swarm of insects flew past the window. In fact, it turned out to be tiny pieces of hay. Some smart arse had decided that it might be fun to push a bundle of hay on the railway line. The train wasn't derailed, but a pipe on the bottom of the engine had broken which translated into major delays. The train could only move at a snail's pace, so we limped to the next station and waited while BR organsised a new engine.

'We arrived at Manchester at 2.50 p.m. Before the train had come to a halt, all the QPR fans were jumping out and putting on a "Linford" to get to the taxis. It was like a scene from *Convoy* with ten to fifteen packed cabs following each other to the ground. We got to our seats two minutes before kickoff. My mate Liam was already sitting in his seat. Having had an extra hour in bed, he still reached Old Trafford half an hour before us! He'd had a relaxed and trouble-free journey on the train after ours.'

In March 1995, a group of 36 Cardiff City fans set out for Plymouth in an independently hired coach. As they were boarding, some of them noticed that they were being watched by police parked up nearby in a van. At about midday, when the coach was approximately eight miles outside of Plymouth, they were confronted by a roadblock of police cars, vans and dogs. Three at a time, they were ordered off the coach. Then they were strip searched and their possessions were confiscated. To their horror, the fans were split up and carted off to police cells in Plymouth, Torquay and Exeter. The supporters who were sent to Exeter had to endure a 45-minute journey in tiny one-man cells inside the police vehicles, before being put in single cells at the police station.

During their time in captivity, the prisoners were let out of their cells once to walk around a yard. They were released at 7.20 p.m. Despite pleas for an explanation, the fans were then given a police escort back to the Severn Bridge, with police cars blocking off motorway exits all the way to Cardiff. The police eventually offered their version of events, claiming that the fans were detained 'on suspicion of a breach of the peace'. Drugs and alcohol had apparently been found on the coach, along with a number of 'calling cards'. Strange, then, that the fans were all released without charge.

When Newcastle United were drawn against Bilbao of Spain in the UEFA Cup in 1994, ex-pat Grimsby fan, Phil Ball, travelled from his home in northern Spain to watch the game. Naturally, he met up with some travelling Geordies before the game, some of whom had a bizarre story to tell. 'I turned to a couple of large Newcastle supporters, already sporting Bilbao shirts,' explains Ball, 'and asked them if they'd been having a decent time. "Good time?" they roared. "This is the best fucking place we've ever been in our lives, man!"'

They then told Ball how they had arrived two days previously in a knackered old van and gone to a garage to ask for a weld for their exhaust pipe. They had had the van completely overhauled and the garage owners had refused to take any payment for the job. Instead, they had been taken to a bar and plied with free drinks for the next two days. One Geordie said, 'It's brilliant, man. They love us here. It's weird.'

Being a British ex-pat abroad can have its drawbacks because high-quality football can sometimes be quite thin on the ground. David Townsend is one such deprived Brit, living in the city of Sendai in northern Japan. His local side play in the Second Division of the 'J' League to a very poor standard, so Townsend was thrilled to discover that the recently built stadium in Sendai was to host an international match – even if it was only between Turkey and Croatia. 'The big day arrived and two months of planning came to fruition,' said Townsend. 'My mates and I set off, red and white painted faces, vast quantities of vodka and orange, parading a huge banner encouraging Asanovic to give us a wave and asking whether his family like squid – it was all we could find in the Croatian phrase book.

'In my excitement, I decided to go early in order to save the seats behind the goal. The Japanese were not going to argue. They just looked bewildered as this mad Englishman swigging orange juice ran round hugging chairs. The lads arrived and it was all going well, but as the game kicked off, the vodka kicked in. After ten minutes I wandered off to the toilets, which were so nice I decided to stop for a little nap. The next thing I recall is my mates climbing over the bog door, picking me up and chucking me out of the stadium.

'I began my dejected stagger home, stopping only to lean against a small barrier. Gravity then played its trump card and I plunged over the barrier and tumbled twenty feet down a grass embankment. Lying in a crumpled heap at the bottom, I began my second nap of the day. I woke to the sound of five or six Japanese people scurrying around me. They lifted me up and carried me back into the stadium to watch the end of a poor 1-1 draw.'

Not to be left out, non-League football has its own stories to tell as well, covering the whole gamut of footballing disasters. A few years ago, London Sunday League side Milldean FC organised an away match at Eton, and as a special treat the players decided to take their wives and children on the coach with them. Milldean won the match but were banned from using the changing rooms after a dispute about tough tackling and an argument with the referee who, Eton claimed, had added on too much injury time. Instead, the Milldean players had to ask permission to change in a pub toilet, which could only lead to disaster. After a few drinks, the players decided they needed to get a closer view of the Thames, which the pub overlooked. The inevitable happened.

'Look! Daddy's jumping off the bridge!' squealed one child.

Other players followed suit, and George Ward (now club secretary) lost his watch in twenty feet of water.

'He'd been proudly showing it off all day. We had to keep diving into that bloody river looking for it,' said Barry Knox, the former club secretary. The watch was never found, leaving Ward to reflect on the possible damage that he could have done to himself. 'After we'd been jumping in the river this old bloke came up to us and said, "You don't want to do that. The kids throw scaffolding poles off the bridge and you'll impale yourself." I thought, Thanks mate. You've been watching us jumping all afternoon!'

Hereford Sunday League side Hearts recently travelled to the Pyrenees for a football tournament and some skiing. The heady combination of a football team, snow and large quantities of aprés-ski drinks proved an explosive one. One player had his hand put in plaster after falling over, while another smashed his face open while skiing off piste. The latter was Luke Gosling, who went on to experience further trauma. 'I also sliced my hand open falling down a massive hill after a few drinks. There was no hospital nearby so we taped it up ourselves. Back home, the doctor said we'd done a decent job, which is amazing really as we were pretty drunk.' No-one talked about the football.

These stories are only the tip of the iceberg but they amply demonstrate the trials and tribulations of supporting a football club. From the comedic to the sad, whoever said that football is a mere reflection of life itself was not far wrong.

8 More Names Withheld to Protect the Guilty

THE PLAYERS CLAMBER ON TO THE TEAM BUS and engage in the usual post-match banter with the driver. The atmosphere is always determined by whether the team has won or lost, and a draw often leaves the atmosphere as nondescript as the match just played. Most clubs are reluctant to swap coach drivers: the trust and camaraderie built up over the season are an important part of match-day rituals. Compared with the superstars they deliver to grounds, coach drivers earn a pittance, and an untrustworthy one could earn significant amounts of extra money selling stories about their clients' high jinks to newspapers.

The media interest that this story could have generated would have been considerable. The players, who shall remain nameless, decided they fancied a one-way bet. Their coach driver was offered a plastic cup containing an international player's urine, a delight to some New Age health freaks but understandably repulsive to this particular driver. The gathered ensemble of stars offered the driver £50 in cash if he drank the contents of the cup. He refused. The ante was raised from £100 to £500 and still he refused . . . until the cash offered totalled £2,500. Unable to say no to such a large increase to his earnings, he gulped the lot down in one. Amidst whoops and cheers, the wad of notes was handed to the driver and he rightfully took his place in football folklore.

Perhaps the lesser of two evils concerns the coach driver who was handcuffed to his steering wheel by a couple of English jolly japesters for the entire match, only to be undone when the team wanted to go home. First stop on the motorway was probably the services to answer the call of nature.

A well-known international striker was accommodated by his new club to a ridiculous degree. To the annoyance of his colleagues, he was mollycoddled, given a beautiful house, had his bills paid – and was paid a fortune to boot. When he left the club, he vacated the house to make way for another international player, who discovered the departing striker had stolen the cutlery!

Any form of racism in football is intolerable. It is bad enough among fans, deplorable between players and extremely alarming if it filters higher up the club pyramid, as it invariably does. One black player was once the subject of a social discussion between several individuals, one of whom held a position of considerable responsibility within the club. The dreadlocked player was described as a 'twiglet-haired cunt' by the club official, and two weeks later player and club decided to go their separate ways. The player concerned now plies his trade elsewhere and is thankfully still unaware of the disparaging way to which he was referred.

The demon drink has been the downfall of many a football personality, some more famous than others. Those who enjoy their drink strive not to let it affect their work but there have been occasions when a penchant for a tipple has led to an embarrassing situation. One coach turned to drink as solace for his team's poor performances and obviously had too much one night as, next day, he threw up on the training pitch in front of his players!

One player, desperate for a cool, refreshing drink at half time, grabbed a bottle in the team dressing room and took a gulp, only to spit it out quickly as it contained cordial and vodka. It emerged that another member of his club kept a half-time pick-me-up in the bottle: the player and the bottle owner still rarely see eye to eye.

An international striker who enjoys many a night out with his entourage decided to make a spectacle of himself in a continental restaurant by standing up at the table and urinating in the ice bucket in full view of the other diners. He then sat down as if nothing had happened and carried on with his meal to the tittering amusement of his friends. Not a word was said to the player by any of the restaurant staff, who tolerate the player's erratic behaviour because of his regular custom.

If the 1996 Hong Kong 'dentist chair' incident was embarrassing for England's international football team, it was also a good reminder of Rule No. 1 in the Footballer's Guide to Conduct – have fun, but not with reporters around.

While on a football tour, one mindless international youth player decided to ingratiate himself to his Malaysian hosts by urinating on the floor of their hotel foyer. A reporter who witnessed the act said that the player showed no remorse and acted in a dismissive, arrogant manner when confronted by irate hotel staff. Despite this appalling episode, he still represents his country at youth level.

By no means is he the only budding star to flirt with lunacy. One now very famous international once rolled around in dog faeces in front of journalists at a prestigious international tournament in 1988. Just *why* he did it is as much a mystery now as it was then.

Another successful British international, on a bender with colleagues to celebrate a big victory, was stuck for transportation back to the team hotel. Pleasantly merry, the players spotted a cab coming down the road and attempted to hail it. When the taxi slowed down to take a better look at the prospective passengers, this particular player jumped on to the bonnet of the taxi and refused to move until the driver accepted his fare. Alcoholic high jinks maybe, but his club would have read him the riot act if they had ever found out.

Not all trips abroad are sleaze laden; some are just hilarious. When the Scottish team flew out together for the 1978 World Cup finals in Argentina, they all travelled on the same plane. When on board the jumbo jet, a large forward (name withheld to prevent further embarrassment) spotted a staircase.

'What's up there?' he asked.

'That,' replied a small, mischievous player (now a manager), 'is the entrance to the snooker room.'

The forward said that he loved snooker and challenged his colleague to a game for a tenner.

The two players agreed that they would have to wait until the seatbelt sign was switched off, and the forward was told, 'We can't play while the plane's climbing – all the balls roll to the bottom cushion.' The jet rose into the air, seatbelts were unfastened and the forward was off. He climbed the stairs two at a time and burst into the peaceful 'bubble' of the jumbo, bellowing, 'Me and [player X] get first go on the snooker table! Right?'

The terrified passengers stared in disbelief while the small mischievous player roared with laughter.

Neutrals on the plane decided that the Scots were not destined to win the 1978 World Cup.

A slightly more serious incident, but none the less just as comical, happened a few years ago at the training ground of a top English club. Adamant that his players should do their fair share of running, the manager used to lambaste them if he felt they were being lazy. On this occasion, he gave his orders and disappeared behind some trees to spy on the players. Unhappy with what he saw, he trotted off to the boot of his car and reappeared near the training pitch some minutes later. Jumping out of some bushes, he fired a shot from a high-powered air rifle into the air, frightening the living daylights out of his players. Strangely, they had no trouble picking up the pace after that.

The power football journalists wield is significant. They can stop damaging stories from going to print, nurture relationships to get exclusive stories and influence public opinion at the stroke of a pen or tap on a computer. Players are suspicious of journalists at best, but some stonewall them completely and others take a great deal of courting to extract the information that a hack requires. In a sense, it's a mutual-abuse society that exists between large sections of the two parties. Favours are frequently done and are called in by return. 'Friendly' journalists are quickly identified by players and managers and they use each other for their own ends. Journalists frequently make the initial enquiries with a club on behalf of players – in fact, before registered agents were introduced, some journalists were already doing the job for free.

It is not unusual for a player to try and influence a

journalist's copy. Over a quiet drink with a seasoned scribe, one international player asked for a story to appear alluding to the fact that a big British club was interested in signing him. The club had been interested some years earlier and the player was keen to rekindle the story for his own ends. The journalist concerned did not print the speculative story and the player still hasn't joined the club.

Several years ago, while working in Norwich, a well-known male entertainer was visited at his hotel by a young man. The entertainer was staying for a few weeks doing pantomime and the young man's visits were fairly frequent. One of the hotel's female receptionists began to take notice of the visitor – she thought she had seen him somewhere before but could not quite recall where.

One evening, the young man signed the visitors' book and all became clear. He was a rising star from the world of football and today is an extremely bankable name in British football. He is married now with a family but has always had something of a playboy image and appealed to young women. Perhaps he was just helping the pantomine star learn his lines.

A leading English club witnessed a player fracas on the training pitch in the 1997/98 season when a senior player decided to berate another established star over his constant whingeing about niggling injuries. The dissatisfaction simmered for quite some time, culminating in the 'whingeing' player being slapped by his colleague. The injured star was backed up by two of his colleagues, who hurled racial abuse and threats at the other player. Both still play for the same team but the manager has now gone. It was claimed that towards the end of his reign, he read a tabloid newspaper in the final minutes before the players left the dressing room, such was his disillusionment with the job.

Of course, the rumour mill is part and parcel of football but it can involve potentially very serious allegations. One of the most talked about areas of football gossip is drug abuse, although thankfully most of the circulating stories are pure fantasy. Nevertheless, rumour inevitably creates doubt, and even your own flesh and blood can become suspicious. One Premier League player rumoured to be a drug user was confronted by his angry father on his doorstep. Before the player could get a word in, his father had punched him in the face and told him that he never wanted to hear stories of him drug taking again, whether true or false.

The 1990s have seen so much money swilling around in football that the critics say the game has lost its soul. The working man's game is no more, they say, swallowed up by corporate entertainment and greedy boards of directors. At one large British club where the balance sheet is more important than the team sheet, players are charged for chewing gum at the training ground and have to fork out for extra isotonic drinks. Another club chose to charge one of its longest-serving players for the corner flags at his testimonial match. If that was not bad enough, they also wanted to deduct £1 for every ticket sold for the game. For the uninitiated, the accepted protocol for testimonial games is that the player gets the use of the stadium from the club and is only expected to meet the cost of policing the event – which is taken care of by his testimonial committee. Nothing else should be chargeable to the player as the game is supposed to be a gift from the club for outstanding long service – usually ten years. The club in question should be ashamed.

Evading trouble both off and on the pitch should be uppermost in every player's mind. As we all know, some are better at it than others. According to the papers, only three or four England players were implicated in the Hong Kong 'dentist chair' incident when the whole team were out on the town. One unlikely (in the general public's eyes) participant was spotted shortly afterwards at Joe Bananas in Hong Kong wearing a ripped, drink-stained shirt and staggering around the bar. The player was never associated with the incident but clearly took part. With the press, there's often one rule for one and one rule for the others.

While abroad, a former British international disappeared with a blonde who worked for the team's sponsors. The married star was gone for nearly two hours and could, of course, have been playing dominoes – not that anyone ever considered that as an option. The next morning, he was quizzed loudly over breakfast and visibly squirmed when he was also asked about his involvement with another girl, well known on the football circuit at the time. He must have nearly choked on his cornflakes.

Half the fun is trying to guess who the offenders are. The sources for the stories are totally confidential and wholly reliable, but are probably just the tip of the iceberg. After all, footballers are only human. Well, most of them, anyway.

9 World Cup Babylon

BEFORE A BALL HAD BEEN KICKED at France 98 this summer, the world's most prestigious sporting event was already embroiled in controversy. The distribution of match tickets not only took on farcical proportions but the back pedalling and mixed messages from the French World Cup organisers exposed the indecision in their ranks. Fans without tickets were invited to France to watch the action on giant screens, segregation appeared to be virtually non-existent and, in Lens, England supporters were to be penned in behind fencing which can only remind them of the bad old days. Not quite the festival of football that we were all expecting.

The protagonists have had their problems too. Colombia's Carlos Valderrama had an early threat of not playing because of an outstanding tax bill, the Brazilians were undergoing 'emotional counselling' to try and retain their trophy, discord in the German and Dutch camps could threaten their challenge and Glenn Hoddle has incurred the wrath of a spoon bender and employed an ex-girlfriend's mother, Eileen Drewery, to sprinkle some mystical 'magic dust' over England's preparations. All this, and the long, arduous qualifying campaign were merely the appetisers for a main course which ultimately looked and probably tasted good but which precipitated one or two bouts of footballing indigestion.

The history of the World Cup is littered with incidents that FIFA would rather forget about, as on and off the pitch the game's bad boys have exercised their less than benevolent ambitions. Diego Maradona was unceremoniously kicked out of USA 94 for playing while under the influence of banned substances. He claimed that he was innocent and the Argentine team doctor concurred, saying that the substances involved were bought over the counter at a drug store in America and therefore must be legal. Maradona returned to Argentina and decided to use an air rifle to take pot shots at a group of journalists waiting outside his Buenos Aires home.

Scotland's Willie Johnson also took an early plane home – from the finals in Argentina in 1978. Johnson was caught taking two pills before Scotland's game with Peru and tested positive after a urine test. The tablets were for hayfever and Johnson later revealed that even though he was not fit to play, pressure from his colleagues forced him to take the medication, which was readily available back in Britain. He was banned for a year by FIFA and condemned by the Scottish Football Association for his actions, a move which convinced him that he was to be the scapegoat. 'All Scotland had to do was appeal and ask for another test, but I've always felt that they were happy to see me out. It meant that they were able to blame someone for all that had gone wrong,' remembers Johnson.

This certainly wasn't the only incident of that year. The 1978 World Cup finals in Argentina were littered with trouble. In fact, Amnesty International urged a complete boycott of the tournament because of Argentina's appalling human rights record. Despite valiant campaigning, the finals went ahead – much to the relief of Argentina's ruling military junta. The terrorist group the Montoneros kindly announced that they would not disrupt the spectacle and described the forthcoming tournament as 'a feast for the people'. In a football-mad country, even terrorists can forget their ideals and principles for the World Cup.

It turned out to be a tournament where Argentine football enjoyed something of a renaissance. The hosts were swept along on a wave of ticker-tape emotion and it must have been hell being a stadium cleaner. But it was in the second series of group games that things started to get interesting, when Brazil faced Poland and Argentina played Peru. Brazil beat Poland 4-1, conveniently alerting the hosts to the exact score they needed to progress in the competition. Argentina had to beat Peru 4-0.

Rumours abounded of underhand goings-on, in which the Argentinians bribed Peru to fix the game. Allegedly, the generals of Peru, running short of money, were only too willing to help and the arrangements were made by Admiral Carlos Lacoste, a World Cup organiser and, at the time, vice-president of FIFA. Argentina shipped 35,000 tons of free grain to Peru and it was rumoured that arms shipments were part of the deal as well. As an added incentive, the Argentinian Central Bank suddenly freed $50 million in credits for Peru. Argentina's manager, Cesar Luis Menotti, barred his goalkeeper and substitutes from his pre-match team talk. In the match itself, Peru played four reserves, a defender up front and their goalkeeper Quiroga (a naturalised Argentinian known as El Loco, the madman) performed more eccentrically than usual. Argentina won 6-0 and reached the final.

In the final itself, intimidation was crudely used in anticipation of victory. Argentina played Holland, a team packed full of skilful artistic players most coaches could only dream of. The hosts deliberately kept the Dutch waiting for five minutes before kickoff, leaving them entirely alone on the pitch in front of 100,000 fanatical, baying Argentinians – not the most sporting and hospitable thing to do. Argentina went on to win the final but the free kick count aroused some suspicion, with referee Sergio Gonell of Italy awarding 46 fouls against Holland and only 20 against Argentina.

Holland had also missed out four years earlier, in 1974, when West Germany hosted the World Cup finals. The much-fancied Dutch, purveyors of 'total football', were among the favourites to lift the trophy, but Germany's best-selling tabloid newspaper, *Bild*, decided to save their biggest World Cup exposé for them, revealing that sex, smoking and alcohol were all allowed in the team hotel. Seemingly intent on unsettling any visiting teams who posed a threat to the hosts, *Bild* suggested that the Dutch were copulating their way to glory. After Holland beat Brazil 2-0 to finish top of Group B, the Dutch players threw a party at their hotel, which ended up in the swimming pool. One female reveller dived in semi-naked and was captured on camera by a Germany partygoer. Predictably, *Bild*'s front page the following day was graced by the unknown woman, and the Dutch players were besieged by phone calls from their wives and girlfriends demanding explanations.

Not to be put off, the Dutch were up to their old tricks again in 1978. Having been defeated by Argentina in the final, the players decided to have a party on board their flight home. Mayhem ensued, with several stewardesses claiming that they were assaulted. Then the players learnt that their flight was due to be met by the queen of Holland as a special welcome home. In no fit state to mix with royalty, they were only saved by a fortunate turn of events when their plane had to refuel in Paris, allowing them a couple of extra hours to sober up.

Sex (or the lack of it) has played its part in World Cup history, with sex-free training camps a particular favourite among coaches. Before the 1974 World Cup finals, the Brazilians were locked away in a month-long, ultra-strict environment supervised by their coach, Mario Zagalo. The enforced celibacy prompted defender Luis Pereira to complain: 'This is supposed to make us world champions. World champions of what? Masturbation?'

After the 1982 finals in Spain, the journalistic grapevine was awash with rumours that two members of the Italian squad were discovered in bed together engaging in a non-heterosexual act. Extremely fortunately, however, Italy won the World Cup that year and the story drifted into obscurity, such is the obsession for football success.

Controversial German goalkeeper Harald Schumacher revealed in his autobiography that during the 1986 World Cup in Mexico, many members of the West Germany team indulged in lurid sex sessions. Highly organised Germans ferried in numerous supervised call girls to the team hotel. Schumacher wrote: 'We were not eunuchs. It's better than letting the young players scurry off to the nearest town and perhaps catch VD and foot and mouth disease in some sleazy brothel.'

This year's finals saw a surfeit of yellow and red cards, as FIFA instructed all referees to adhere strictly to their directives. But quite how a current referee would have dealt with 'The Battle of Santiago' in 1962 remains open to question. Host nation Chile met Italy on 2 June but before a ball was kicked bad feeling between the two sides had become more than apparent. The Chileans resented the poaching of their players by Italian clubs and the situation wasn't helped by a couple of very disparaging articles about Chile in the newspapers.

English referee Ken Aston struggled to control the most vicious match in World Cup history. After eight minutes of play, Giorgio Ferrini was sent off for kicking Chile's Landa. However, he refused to leave the pitch and the referee, at his wits' end, summoned the police to forcibly march Ferrini away. A young David Coleman commented on BBC television: 'This is one of the sorriest, stupidest spectacles I've ever seen.'

Five minutes before half time, Chile retaliated when Leonel Sanchez, the son of a boxer, punched and broke Limberto Maschio's nose. Amazingly, Aston and his linesmen did not see the incident, but David Coleman certainly spotted it. 'That was one of the neatest left hooks I've ever seen. It's the most appalling, disgusting and disgraceful game of football ever played.'

A few minutes later, with Sanchez now a marked man, Italy's Mario David attempted to kick him in the head. He missed but executed a perfect drop kick to his neck. He was rewarded with a red card and Chile won 2-0. [Ratin and his 1966 Argentinian thugs were angels by comparison, but at the time Alf Ramsey branded the team 'animals' and the England players refused to swap shirts with them.]

Chile were banned from the 1994 World Cup finals after Chilean goalkeeper Rojas claimed that he had been struck by a flare while playing in a crucial qualifying game against

Brazil. Chile were losing 1-0 and, if the score stayed that way, they would be eliminated. After 65 minutes, Rojas played injured and got himself stretchered off, with Chile refusing to play on. It later transpired that Rojas had inflicted the injuries on himself in a bid to get FIFA to reverse the result. FIFA took a very dim view of the incident, particularly when they discovered that Rojas had been aided and abetted by Chile's manager, physio and team doctor. On top of Chile's disqualification, all the perpetrators were banned by FIFA.

Match fixing is very difficult to prove but sometimes it is more obvious than others. Who could ever forget the farcical 1982 World Cup match between West Germany and Austria? It was the final Group Two qualifying match and both sides' fate rested on the outcome. West Germany needed to win but a 1-0 vistory would see both sides progressing to the next round. The Germans scored early on and Austria made no attempt to score for the rest of the match. The Germans chose to pose and posture their way through the remainder of the game. The facts spoke for themselves and FIFA turned a blind eye.

Football's ruling body wasn't exactly falling over itself to investigate bribery claims by the Poles in the 1974 World Cup. Poland played Italy in Stuttgart, with Italy needing to draw to stay in the competition. Polish coach Gorski claimed that well-heeled Italian supporters tried, with success, to bribe his players. After the competition, several Polish players claimed that they had been offered thousands of dollars a man to lose or draw the game – by the Italian players. Allegations were further made in 1980 by former Polish players, who said that money to throw the game was offered by six Italians in the grandstand who weren't on the bench that day. A suggestion was made at half time, in the dressing rom, that a 2-2 draw would be a very good result. Italy lost 2-1 and FIFA refused to investigate the claims, saying it was strange that the Poles were willing to talk about the events some six years after the incident and not at the time.

The rather extreme theory that international football is merely a substitute for war was amply demonstrated in 1969, when a battle broke out between bitter South American rivals Honduras and El Salvador. The soccer war kicked off officially on 14 July, but the trouble really started on Saturday 7 June when the El Salvador squad arrived in the Honduran capital, Tegucigalpa, for the first match of three in the World Cup play-offs.

Both nations had a history of intense rivalry – notably over land disputes – stretching back over many years. The first match was played on a Sunday, meaning that the El Salvador players had to endure a night of Honduran hospitality. Home fans laid siege to the opposition's hotel, beeped car horns, threw stones at the windows and made makeshift drums from empty barrels. They set off firecrackers and whistled, screamed and chanted all night long. El Salvador weren't exactly at the peak of their game the next day, but held out until the last minute, when Honduran striker Roberto Cardona scored the decisive goal.

Exactly a week later, the Honduran squad arrived in San Salvador for the second match and were transported to their hotel in a fleet of armoured cars to protect them from a baying mob intent on revenge. A screaming crowd surrounded the Hondurans' hotel, shouting, breaking windows and pelting the building with rotten eggs and dead rats.

The following morning the armoured cars returned to ferry

the players and officials to the Flor Blanca Stadium for the match. The army surrounded the ground and inside the *Guardia Nacional* brandished trouble-deterring sub-machine guns. The pre-match build-up included the ceremonial burning of the Honduran flag. El Savador won 3-0 and the victory celebrations were wild, prompting Mario Griffen, the Honduras coach, to comment, 'We're awfully lucky we lost.' The team were escorted back to the airport but their fans weren't so lucky and were brutally attacked. Hundreds were injured and two were killed. More than 150 Honduran cars were burnt out and, hours later, the shared border between the two countries was closed. The repercussions continued with the repatriation of immigrants, extradition orders and streams of refugees as the dispute escalated to government level.

On the eve of the third and deciding match, El Salvador broke off all diplomatic relations with Honduras. This served to fire up the fans even more and it was decided that the third game should be switched to Mexico City. An incredible 5,000 Mexican riot police kept the peace during the match, which turned out to be a classic, ending 3-2 to El Salvador, who qualified for the 1970 World Cup finals in Mexico. Surprisingly, there was no real trouble immediately after the match, but two weeks later El Salvador and Honduras were at war. Hostilities began when El Salvador invaded Honduras and, as in the football, their bigger and better-equipped army took an early lead, breaking through the Honduran defences almost at will.

The fighting raged for over four days. Honduran bombers destroyed El Salvador's oil refineries, leading to the conflict paralysing the central American economic common market. Eventually, the Organisation of American States negotiated a cease-fire but not before 3,000 people had lost their lives and over 100,000 were left homeless. El Salvador were humiliated in the World Cup finals and gained nothing through going to war. There were long-standing political reasons behind 'the sector war', but football was the catalyst for the hostilities. What a shame they couldn't settle the whole affair with a penalty shoot-out.

Italy's national team were accused by an anonymous source of trying to bribe Cameroon to fix a match in the 1982 World Cup. Italy made a very bad start in the tournament but a 1-1 draw with Cameroon was enough to send them through to the second stage. If Cameroon had won, they would have gone through at Italy's expense. Among the players said to have accepted money was Roger Milla. Italy and Milla vociferously denied the accusation and FIFA decided there was no case to answer.

Middle Eastern passions for football tend to run high, especially if the game concerned is a World Cup qualifying game with a near neighbour. In late 1985, Iraq's leading sports newspaper printed the following command on the morning of a vital match between Iraq and Syria: 'In case of loss, God forbid, the people will not stand idle but will pelt those who disappoint their hopes with tomatoes and bottles.' The Iranian newspaper front pages will be worth reading on the day they play America in France 98.

Much-fancied Colombia failed to live up to their star billing during USA 94 and one player paid the ultimate price for the failure. Sweeper Andrew Escobar managed to score an own goal against the United States and incurred the wrath of the drug cartels and their organised betting syndicates who had made very heavy wagers on Colombia's success. Upon the team's return to Colombia, Escobar was shot twelve times by a smiling assassin in the Las Palmas suburb of Medillin. Within days, two petty gangsters, Munoz Castro and Santiago Gallon Henao, were arrested and eventually convicted of the murder, but few people believed the government's claim that the murder of Escobar was not linked to the cartels. In short, he was a scapegoat.

The Albanians will forever hold a special place in World Cup history and by the same token will be remembered for the most embarrassing football faux pas. In 1989, the Albanians flew in from Tirana for a World Cup qualifying game against England at Wembley which they lost. However, the squad were obviously impressed by London and all that it had to offer. Before their flight, they decided to go to the duty free shop and several players were soon apprehended by police after stocking up with just about everything they could lay their hands on. None of the goods had been paid for as the Albanians had interpreted the word 'free' and taken its meaning literally. They were all let off without charge and sent on their way.

While football may be a team game, there are always those individuals who stand out – and the World Cup is no exception, as the following stories demonstrate.

Jose Batista was sent off after 55 seconds while playing for Uruguay and against Scotland in 1986. The lengths some people will go to avoid playing the Scots . . .

In September 1995, Oussama Aytour, star of the Lebanese World Cup squad, was fined £300 after magistrates found him guilty of making an explosive device at his brother's flat in Fulham. Aytour, who was visiting London at the time, told police that he had got bored while everybody was out and had made the device for fun. He told the court, 'I meant no harm. I just wanted to amuse myself.'

Polish coach Jacek Gmoch decreed that during the 1978 World Cup he didn't mind his players drinking and smoking but he drew the line at indulging during games. Gmoch ordered 380 bottles of vodka to be laid on at the Polish team headquarters in time for the start of the competition's second phase. No wonder they were knocked out.

Gazza would have appreciated such a gesture. He bribed the waiters at England's Sardinian HQ in 1990 to top up his mineral water with white wine.

Colombian coach Pacho Maturana dismissed claims by the press that his players, while in America for USA 94, were serial womanisers. He admitted that during the tournament certain players engaged in sex sessions but only with women of 'good quality', as he put it.

During the 1978 finals in Argentina, the hosts' 'win at all costs' mentality knew no bounds. Several players claimed that their Argentinian counterparts seemed extremely excitable during games, and two of Argentina's star players – Mario Kempas and Alberto Tarantini – were so hyper after playing one World Cup match that they had to keep exercising for an hour after the final whistle in order to come down again. Maybe it was fortunate that FIFA's dope-testing methods were not as sophisticated as they are today.

In a recent World Cup, a ball boy's pregnant girlfriend was allegedly recruited by a top side to provide urine for a drugs test. The team involved were deeply concerned that the player picked out for a random drugs test would have tested positive. Large sums of money almost certainly changed hands.

The fans don't escape either.

A poverty stricken Albanian wagered his wife on the outcome of the 1994 game between Argentina and Bulgaria.

Not only did he lose the bet but he lost his wife as well. She left him for the winner of the bet.

In 1997, an anonymous United Arab Emirates fan offered the referee a £25,000 bung before his team's World Cup qualifier against Japan. The Costa Rican official declined the offer and the game ended 1-1.

Seventeen-year-old Chinese fan Xia Qian Li strangled his father because he wasn't allowed to watch the opening ceremony of the 1990 World Cup in Italy. Perhaps a slight overreaction but then, football always has been a game of high emotions, and despite the sleaze and scandal, it's still the most exciting sport in the world.